CELEBRATED PETS

Endearing Tales of Companionship and Loyalty

CHERYL MACDONALD

VICTORIA · VANCOUVER · CALGARY

Heritage House Publishing Company Ltd.
#108 – 17665 66A Avenue
Surrey, BC V3S 2A7
www.heritagehouse.ca

Heritage House Publishing Company Ltd.
PO Box 468
Custer, WA
98240-0468

Library and Archives Canada Cataloguing in Publication
MacDonald, Cheryl, 1952 –
    Celebrated pets: endearing tales of companionship and loyalty / Cheryl MacDonald.

ISBN 978-1-894974-81-3

    1. Pets—Canada—Biography. 2. Human-animal relationships—Canada—History. 3. Famous animals—Canada. I. Title.

SF411.36.C3M33 2009   636.088'70971   C2008-908129-3

Originally published 2006 by Altitude Publishing Canada Ltd.

Library of Congress Control Number: 2009920309

Series editor: Lesley Reynolds.
Cover design: Chyla Cardinal. Interior design: Frances Hunter.
Cover photo: National Archives of Canada (PA-150000). Interior photos: National Gallery of Canada, page 12 (William Berczy); Centre for Newfoundland Studies Archives, Memorial University, page 30; Getty Images, page 37 (3330437); Archives of Manitoba, page 49 (N10467; Colebourn, D. Harry 9) and page 54 (N10468; Colebourn, D. Harry 10); British Columbia Archives, page 61 (F-07888), page 63 (F-07756) and page 68 (B-02224); London Stereoscopic Company/Stringer); National Archives of Canada, page 75 (PA-147585) and page 92 (PA-174058).

Mixed Sources
Cert no. SW-COC-001271
© 1996 FSC
FSC

The interior of this book was printed on 100% post-consumer recycled paper, processed chlorine free and printed with vegetable-based inks.

Heritage House acknowledges the financial support for its publishing program from the Government of Canada through the Book Publishing Industry Development Program (BPIDP), Canada Council for the Arts and the province of British Columbia through the British Columbia Arts Council and the Book Publishing Tax Credit.

BRITISH COLUMBIA
ARTS COUNCIL

The Canada Council | Le Conseil des Arts
for the Arts | du Canada

12 11 10 09   1 2 3 4 5

Printed in Canada

In memory of cherished canine companions
Brandy, King, Smokey, Tammy, Molly, Jake and Buster

Contents

Prologue

WINTER HAD ALREADY ARRIVED IN *Quebec when Grey Owl and his wife, Anahareo, set out to their new cabin. After sending most of their equipment by sleigh, they loaded their canoe with camping gear and their beloved beaver kittens, McGinnis and McGinty. Now eight months old, the kittens travelled in a portable stove—basically a rectangular metal box—for safety. On this trip there was an extra reason to keep them confined. The kittens, who had been dubbed "The Macs," had lost much of their fur to a mysterious ailment. While a change of diet and some salve seemed to be working, in their hairless condition they were vulnerable to the penetrating cold of icy waters.*

The Macs protested with an assortment of squawks and

grumblings. Grey Owl and Anahareo ignored them, paddling as swiftly as possible toward their destination. The sides and bottom of the canoe became coated with ice, but Grey Owl was an experienced canoeist. Standing on the slippery stern, he poled hard into the water. "In an especially stiff piece of fast water," Grey Owl later wrote, "my moccasins, frozen and slippery as glass, shot from under me on the icy canoe bottom and I fell flat on my face in the river." The shift in balance tipped the canoe on its side. Anahareo, who had been kneeling in the canoe, was flung into the water. Moments later, the pair was standing upright in the river, horrified to realize the stove and the beaver kittens were somewhere in the icy water. Shut tight in their stove, with no possibility of escape, the Macs would drown or freeze within minutes. Grey Owl and Anahareo groped frantically beneath the surface. "Suddenly we were holding up the dripping stove between us, although we could never remember the act of finding it, and Anahareo was crying out, 'They're alive! they're alive!'"

1

Pets from the Past

IN 1642, FRENCH COLONISTS ESTABLISHED Ville-Marie, a new settlement on the St. Lawrence River. The settlers who began the community that is now Montreal had a very difficult time at first. There were the usual hardships involved in carving a new life from the wilderness—stretching out supplies brought from Quebec City or France, building shelters, raising crops and coping with the extremes of the Canadian climate. Worst of all was the presence of the Iroquois, who were determined to drive out the French by any means possible.

Knowing that the settlers were greatly outnumbered, the authorities of Ville-Marie made good use of the dogs brought from France to guard cattle. On March 30, 1644, according to the *Jesuit Relations*, the dogs began "to cry out and howl with all their might, looking towards the direction where they sensed the enemy." Alerted to the presence of the Iroquois, about 30 settlers marched out to meet them. Although the settlers were ultimately forced to retreat, the skirmish kept the Native warriors away from the tiny settlement.

By 1647, hostilities had escalated. To combat the Iroquois threat, the colony's leader, Paul de Chomedey, Sieur de Maisonneuve, brought in some reinforcements from France. Among them was Raphaël-Lambert Closse, who became the sergeant-major of the village garrison and took over the leadership of the fledgling colony whenever Maisonneuve was away.

Closse owned a bitch named Pilote, who was considered the most remarkable dog in Ville-Marie, and was even described in detail by the missionary Jérôme Lalemant in the *Jesuit Relations*. Like many dogs, Pilote loved squirrel hunting, but what amazed the settlers were her daily routine and her alertness. Every morning, without fail, she patrolled the village, usually with her pups trailing behind her. "If one of them was stubborn she would bite it to keep going; furthermore, if one turned back in their hunt she would punish the puppy at their return. If she found any Iroquois, she ran directly home barking and letting people from the Fort know that the enemy was not far." Her repeated warnings helped the struggling colony survive in the face of fierce odds.

How long Pilote lived is not known. Her abilities and the colonists' admiration for her were remarkable, but Montreal's earlier chroniclers had more important matters to consider. However, Pilote's reputation became part of local legend, as did that of her master. On February 6, 1662, when 200 Iroquois attacked settlers near Montreal, Closse led a small band of men to rescue them and was killed in the ensuing fight. His funeral eulogy was recorded for posterity in the *Relations*. "He was a man whose piety was no whit inferior to his valour, and who possessed extraordinary presence of mind in the heat of battle ... Montreal owes him its life." In addition, many believed that Montreal owed its life to Pilote and the other dogs who were the first line of defence against hostile Iroquois.

The memory of both Closse and Pilote survived for more than two centuries. In 1892, to celebrate Montreal's 250th anniversary, plans were drawn up to erect a statue in Maisonneuve's honour in Place d'Armes. At each corner of the statue's base were sculptures of individuals who figured prominently in the city's history. Raphaël-Lambert Closse is at the southeastern corner, his pistol drawn and a strained, alert expression on his face. Pressed against his left side, wearing an equally alert expression and restrained by her master's arm, is Pilote.

Like Pilote, the earliest dogs and cats that reached Canada were regarded more as work animals than as pets. They had a purpose, whether it was guarding against

Berczy's 1809 portrait of the Woolsey family of Montreal included their pet dog.

invaders, herding cattle, pulling sleds or killing rodents. But many developed close bonds with their humans. If the animals' names and activities are not recorded, it is because of early Canadians' lower levels of literacy and preoccupation with survival, not their lack of affection for dogs, cats and other pets.

Historical accounts are filled with references to these animals, although in many instances the stories are maddeningly short on detail. For centuries, dogs and cats had been so much a part of Canadians' lives that they were often taken for granted. Domesticated dogs probably arrived in Canada along with the first human immigrants. And the ancestors of Native Americans, who some scholars believe crossed the Bering Strait land bridge during the last ice age, undoubtedly travelled with dogs, some of which may have evolved into the Tahltan bear dog. Now virtually extinct, it is one of the four breeds of truly Canadian dogs, along with the Nova Scotia duck tolling retriever, Eskimo husky and Newfoundland dog. Later, Viking explorers brought their own canine companions, as did the Portuguese and Basque fishermen who visited the Grand Banks prior to 1500. Cats may also have accompanied these fishermen in order to keep the rat population of their ships at manageable levels.

In the first years of settlement, few people had the time or the education to record observations or feelings about their own—or other people's—pets. When they did write about dogs, cats or other animals, they displayed a range of attitudes. Often, their behaviour towards their companion animals was extremely harsh by modern standards. Even some of the most indulgent animal lovers thought nothing of beating a dog to make it obey or instigating animals to fight with each other. But physical violence against people was also extremely common at the time. Husbands hit wives, parents beat children and teachers strapped students, usually without a second thought, because corporal punishment was considered necessary to overcome humans' "animal" instincts and turn them into respectable members of society. It is not surprising that the treatment of animals reflected this prevailing philosophy.

Early Canadian settlers portrayed their pets as cherished companions, annoying pests, protectors, beasts of burden or even potential food sources. Sometimes the animals filled multiple roles, such as the Moodie family pig, Spot, who was lavished with love for weeks before ending up on the dinner table. Because their own lives were often precarious, it was fairly common for early Canadians to ignore dogs and cats, or to view them as dispensable. And yet there were always some who bonded with their animal companions, took pleasure in their antics and memorialized them in writing.

Dogs show up in historical records more than cats do, probably because they were considered more valuable as guards or hunters. Nevertheless, there is ample evidence that cats were treasured by early Canadians. Their chief duty was to minimize the depredations of mice and rats, but they also served as companions, as an account written by Amelia Ryerse Harris indicates. Amelia's parents settled in Port Ryerse, on Lake Erie, in the early 1800s. One day, her little brother George went missing. When his hat turned up in the creek, Amelia's mother, Sarah, assumed the worst. As her husband, Samuel, probed the creek with a long pole, expecting the toddler's body to rise to the surface at any moment, Sarah sat stunned on the bank. Then she heard a little voice call, "Mamma," from across the creek, "And there was George, with his little bare head peeping through the bushes with his pet cat by his side."

That cat, or one of its ancestors, probably accompanied the Ryerses from New Brunswick when they moved to Upper Canada. And who knows, perhaps another ancestor originated in New Jersey—the home the family left following the American Revolution—packed into a basket for safekeeping as the refugee Loyalists trekked to their new homes. In some cases, those émigré cats were brought along for companionship, although it went without saying that they were also valuable as mousers. The line between friendship and function was often blurred.

Patrick Campbell, for instance, doted on his dog, but still relied on him for protection against bears and other wild animals. Campbell, who had been a soldier in continental Europe and a forester in his native Scotland, arrived in Saint John, New Brunswick, on August 28, 1791. He promptly set out to explore the wilderness with a dog, a gun and a servant. Determined to write a detailed account of his travels, Campbell kept a careful record, which included several mentions of the dog, "who was not only a staunch and excellent pointer, but had been bred and accustomed to all the kinds of game found in the mountains and woods of Scotland."

A small, light-coloured animal with dark, floppy ears, the dog repeatedly ran off after any scent that intrigued him. "I had constantly to call on him to keep him in, lest a Bear should spring out of the wood on me in his absence," Campbell wrote. However, the dog proved his worth when

Campbell camped in the woods on October 7. All night long the dog barked, and "seemed to have some large animal at bay, which he durst not attack, probably a Bear." Campbell made it through the night unscathed.

Part of Campbell's journey was overland, but he also travelled part of the way by a birchbark canoe "that could hardly carry my Dog besides the poleman, or navigator and myself." Along the waterways, the dog found a beaver lodge to explore and also fought with a mink, sustaining several bites before Campbell's servant shot the mink.

By the second week of October, the ground was covered with snow. At one point, the group portaged through such rough country that the dog, who was already "fatigued, cut, and bruised," had little energy to go chasing after game. Once they were back in the canoe, the dog was able to rest, and a few days later was up to his old tricks again, chasing game at every opportunity.

The dog's single-mindedness almost proved his undoing as they crossed the mountains separating New Brunswick and Quebec. Catching the scent of a deer, the dog took off. Campbell and his servant waited for him to return, then, reasoning that the dog could track them as well as he could track a deer, decided to continue. As the hours passed and no dog appeared, the two men became concerned. By this time, the men had gone so far that they could not return for him, even if they could remember the spot where the dog had gone off after the deer. Both men were distraught. "My poor Dog," wrote Campbell, "who had been my faithful companion and friend, if I may use the expression, for years in all my hunting excursions and travels, kept me from my usual rest, and when he did not appear next morning I despaired of ever seeing him again." Meanwhile, Campbell's servant was close to tears.

But they had underestimated the little dog's determination. A few hours later, he caught up with them. "When he came up to us, after being twenty-four hours absent, with inexpressible joy at finding us, I believe each of us felt as much pleasure as the Dog himself."

Another hardy hunter who became very attached to his dog was William Pope. An English naturalist, painter and farmer who settled near Long Point on Lake Erie, Pope had a series of dogs throughout his lifetime. Among them was Pinto, an English retriever he brought to Canada in 1833. On July 29, 1845, Pope confided to his diary: "Buried my old Dog Pinto—having previously become very infirm and wasted to a mere shadow with sores and disease—the old fellow was about 12 years of age, 11 of which he had been in my possession—twice crossed the Atlantic—excellent in the field—a capital retriever, tender mouthed—a good water dog & very sagacious." Like many early settlers, Pope was deeply attached to the dog who had shared with him the adventure of immigration and pioneer farming.

John William Meyer also bonded with his dog, although his reasons may have been more practical than sentimental. During the American Revolution, Meyer, a farmer from the area of Albany, New York, decided to join the British cause. He set out from Albany to meet troops led by Major-General John Burgoyne, which were then marching through upper New York. Accompanying Meyer were his dog and his brother-in-law.

Before they found Burgoyne's company, the dog collapsed from exhaustion. Rather than abandon him, Meyer picked him up and carried him. Meyer still had some distance to go, and he was tired from the journey. It might have been easier to leave the dog behind, but this Meyer refused to do. When his brother-in-law commented on his devotion to the animal, Meyer responded wryly, "We may have to eat him yet."

He was only half-joking. From time to time, Native people, soldiers, explorers and others had no choice but to eat their dogs or horses. During the American Revolution, John McDonnell, a Scottish immigrant, was one of those fighting against the rebels. In June 1780, McDonnell and other Butler's Rangers attempted to bring a group of Oneida allies through enemy territory to the Niagara area, where many refugees were gathered. McDonnell was ill with rheumatism and ague, and the mission was a failure. To make matters worse, supplies ran out and, according to Walter Butler, the rangers "killed their Horses and Dogs for food." It was an act of desperation that must have troubled many of the men, especially those who felt affection for the animals that had shared their adventures. But in the bitter days of the Revolutionary War, survival was paramount, and only through the deaths of horses and dogs were the rangers able to survive.

Eating dog or horse meat was an extreme measure that most European settlers preferred to avoid. In the case of McDonnell and his companions, the animals saved their lives. Francis Joseph Fitzgerald was not so lucky. An inspector with the Royal Northwest Mounted Police (RNWMP), Fitzgerald had earned a reputation as a resourceful and courageous officer. In 1910, he was asked to lead a patrol from Fort McPherson to Dawson to deliver mail and dispatches. Fitzgerald left Fort McPherson on December 21, 1910, with two other RNWMP constables, George Kinney and Richard Taylor. Samuel Carter, a former constable, came along to guide the men to Dawson.

The small party made two mistakes. Fitzgerald, like many of the early RNWMP officers, was extremely competitive and wanted to break the existing record for the 756-kilometre journey between the two points. To maximize speed, he reduced the supplies the group carried on their dogsleds. The second mistake was having Carter as a guide. Carter had travelled the route just once, and in the other direction, from Dawson to Fort McPherson.

The journey was difficult from the outset, slowed by heavy snow and frigid temperatures. When Carter could not find the trail across the Richardson Mountains, the men wasted nine days looking for the route before reluctantly turning back on January 18. Still, they were plagued by bad luck. Snowstorms hid their tracks, making it difficult to find their way back to the fort. As their supplies dwindled, they were forced to eat their dogs. Eight of the 15 dogs had been slaughtered for food by February 1. The men were suffering terribly, as Fitzgerald noted in his diary. "Skin peeling off our faces and parts of the body, and lips all swollen and split. I suppose this is caused by feeding on dog meat."

In fact, the combined effects of starvation, dehydration, frostbite and exhaustion were taking their toll. On February 5, Fitzgerald wrote in his diary for the last time. They were 115 kilometres from Fort McPherson, with just five dogs left, and were so feeble they could walk only a few kilometres a day. Still, they struggled on for another week, but sometime between February 12 and February 18, all four members of the Lost Patrol perished. Their bodies were discovered a month later, just a few kilometres from Fort McPherson.

While they might have resorted to eating their dogs out of necessity, early settlers generally placed a high value on them, so much so that some men were provoked to violence if their dogs were harmed. In 1706, when Étienne de Véniard de Bourgmond was acting commander of the French fort at Detroit, he fatally wounded an Ottawa after the Native man struck his dog. The incident added to serious tensions between the French and Ottawas.

Eighty years later, the death of another dog played a role in a clash between Native and European cultures. In May 1786, William Harboard and David Nelson were fishing on the Saint John River in New Brunswick. The Loyalist settlers, both of whom had served in the Queen's Rangers, heard dogs barking in the direction of Nelson's house. When they reached it, they saw that several hogs had disappeared and two dogs were attacking the remaining pig. They shot one dog and the other ran off. Jumping to the conclusion that the pigs had been stolen and taken away by boat, the men headed for the river where they saw two Native people in a canoe. They ordered them to stop. "You have got my hogs!" Nelson shouted.

"No," came the reply from the canoe. "You have killed my dog." Nelson and Harboard fired toward the boat, aiming over the heads of the passengers. Then Nelson fired a second time, killing Pierre Benoît before his horrified wife. Both men subsequently appeared in court at the first murder trial in Fredericton, and despite strong racial prejudice against Native peoples, they were convicted. Because he had not done any harm, Harboard was pardoned, but David Nelson was hanged on June 23.

Clearly, both Bourgmond and Pierre Benoît thought highly of their dogs. Another early settler who had a close relationship with his pet was Toussaint Cartier. Known as the hermit of Saint-Barnabé, Quebec, he lived on an island near Rimouski from about 1727 until 1767. Somewhat eccentric, Cartier suffered from epilepsy and other health problems. One of his eyes bulged out of its socket, causing him great pain. Cartier lessened his discomfort by having his dog lick the eye.

The close bond between Cartier and his dog was sufficiently noteworthy to be recorded. And so was the bond between Susanna Moodie's daughter, their family dog and a pet pig. The pioneer author of *Roughing It in the Bush*, Susanna wrote about Spot, a young pig who was given to her daughter Katie in the fall of 1836. The little pig was a great favourite with the household, especially the children, who fed him at the door of the cabin, just like a dog. Even the Moodies' "noble hound," Hector, became fond of Spot. "Spot always shared with Hector the hollow log which served him for a kennel, and we often laughed to see Hector lead Spot around the clearing by his ear."

That winter was a difficult one for the Moodies. As the cold intensified, the household ran out of many supplies. There was no meat, and the Moodies were growing ill on a diet of bad potatoes and bread. Susanna later wrote, "We began—that is, the elders of the family—to cast very hungry eyes upon Spot; but no one liked to propose having him killed." Finally, Jacob, the hired man, broached the subject, pointing out that everyone was weak from lack of food and that it was senseless to keep the pig under the circumstances. Susanna's husband, John, agreed and, "in spite of the tears and prayers of Katie, her uncouth pet was sacrificed to the general want of the family." Spot was slaughtered to provide the family with badly needed protein. But Katie refused to touch the meat, as did the noble Hector. "That dog do teach uz [sic] Christians a lesson how to treat our friends," Jacob told the Moodies at one meal. To prove his point, he offered Hector a rib of fresh pork. Susanna recalled:

The dog turned away with an expression of aversion, and, on a repetition of the act, walked away from the table.

Human affection could scarcely have surpassed the love felt by this poor animal for his playfellow. His attachment to Spot, that could overcome the pangs of hunger—for, like the rest of us, he was half-starved—must have been strong indeed.

While Susanna could express admiration for Hector, other pets caused a bit of consternation in the Moodie household. Susanna kept a cat, Peppermint, even though John was not particularly fond of cats and resented Peppermint's habit of sleeping with them. Emilia, a friend and neighbour of the Moodies, also had a cat, a large tom that was particularly irksome. The tom regarded the Moodie cabin as part of his own territory. He often visited at night, pushing out a wooden shingle that covered a missing pane in the cabin window, then scouring around for something to eat. Once satisfied, he would fall asleep in any spot that caught his fancy, including the pot the Moodies used for cooking potatoes. John Moodie found him there one morning and was so disgusted that he threatened to kill the cat if he saw him near the house again.

When the 1837 Rebellion broke out, John was among the men who went to the defence of Upper Canada. While he was away, the Moodies' youngest son fell ill and Susanna had to look after him around the clock. Tending to her son night after night soon depleted her supply of candles, the only means of lighting the cabin. When she was down to her last candle, with no money to buy more, she left her son in the care of her servant and went to borrow a candle from a neighbour. Susanna had often complained when others borrowed from her, and she hated to ask for anything herself, but had no choice in the matter. The neighbour gladly loaned her last candle—but asked Susanna to bring it back if she did not use it.

By the time Susanna returned home, her son seemed to have improved. As night fell, a large moon rose, giving her enough light to watch over him. She sent her servant to bed, telling her that if the boy seemed worse Susanna would get up and light the candle. Then she stretched out on the bed beside him. Susanna was dozing when she heard the wooden shingle pushed out of the window. Susanna wrote:

> The thought instantly struck me that it was Tom and that, for lack of something better, he might steal my precious candle.
>
> I sprang up from the bed, just in time to see him dart through the broken window, dragging the long white candle after him. I flew to the door, and pursued him half over the field, but all to no purpose. I can see him now, as I saw him then, scampering away for dear life, with his prize trailing behind him, gleaming like a silver tail in the bright light of the moon.

2

Notable Newfies

IN 1841, SIR RICHARD HENRY BONNYCASTLE visited Niagara Falls. Accompanying the Kingston-based soldier and author was Mr. Caesar, a large Newfoundland dog. Bonnycastle and his dog watched men spear fish from the quick-flowing Niagara River as the falls thundered above them. Mr. Caesar became so absorbed in the activities that he slipped from the rocks into the racing water.

"He was swept round and round by the eddies for a long while," Bonnycastle later wrote, "and then carried into the boiling surge of the foamy current, which drove him rapidly down the river for about a mile." The rapid current had claimed lives in the past, and for a time it seemed Mr. Caesar would become another victim. Fortunately, a good-natured ferryman went after the dog, crossing over to the US side of the river to retrieve him. By this time, Mr. Caesar had made his way to shallow water, but he was happy to be hauled into the ferryman's boat.

No one is positive about the origins of Newfoundland dogs. Some say Newfies were descended from animals brought to the east coast of Canada by Vikings around AD 1000. Centuries later, Basque and Portuguese fishermen brought along other large dogs, which also became ancestors of the modern breed. Eventually, the Newfoundland dog evolved. Typically large, black and web-footed, they were prized for their courage, gentleness and devotion, as well as for the swimming ability and strength that made them outstanding work dogs.

By the late 1700s, Newfoundland dogs were well known in Britain and Western Europe. Poets, statesmen and explorers intrigued by the dogs' exotic appearance adopted Newfies as pets. They also became a favourite subject for many artists, and throughout the early 1800s there are numerous references to them in published accounts of exploration and pioneer settlements in North America.

Soon after he arrived in Upper Canada, Lieutenant-Governor John Graves Simcoe obtained a Newfoundland named Jack Sharp from a farmer in the Niagara area. The dog was a great favourite with the Simcoe children as well as with the governor himself, even though Jack came close to upsetting canoes a number of times when the family was travelling on Ontario's waterways.

In February 1793, when Simcoe and his party headed west to examine the proposed site of the provincial capital at the forks of the Thames River, Jack accompanied them. The dog enjoyed tramping through wintry fields around present-day London, Ontario, although he annoyed the lieutenant-governor's Native companions by repeatedly startling game. Jack's antics got him into trouble when he flushed out a porcupine and had to have several quills removed.

Explorers were also known to choose Newfoundlands as their companions. Map-maker and explorer David Thompson took a Newfie with him in his extensive travels, and Americans Lewis and Clark were accompanied by Seaman, a Newfoundland dog, on their famous trek to the Pacific in 1802.

Both Catharine Parr Traill and Susanna Moodie, pioneer sisters who wrote extensively about the backwoods of Upper Canada, were familiar with Newfoundland dogs. Writing about a pioneer concert in *Life in the Clearings, Versus the Bush*, Susanna Moodie describes how a song about "the drowning child saved by the Newfoundland dog" drew a hearty round of applause. That very subject was depicted in 1856 when noted British artist Sir Edwin Landseer painted *Saved*, a sentimental scene of a black-and-white Newfoundland hovering protectively over a young child he has just saved from drowning.

Landseer completed several paintings featuring Newfoundland dogs, usually the black-and-white variety that now bears his name. The breed became so popular for its characteristic devotion and gentleness that when J.M. Barrie wrote *Peter Pan* in 1904, he made Nana, the dog who served as nurse to the Darling children, a Newfoundland dog. (Nana was transformed into a St. Bernard in the Disney film version of *Peter Pan*.)

Perhaps the most famous Newfoundland dog of all belonged to celebrated romantic poet George Gordon, Lord Byron. As famous for his extravagant lifestyle as he was for his work, Byron scandalized polite society with his outrageous behaviour and romantic liaisons. But he was also a great lover of animals.

The only son of a mentally unstable Scottish mother and a wastrel father, he had started life in genteel poverty, but Byron eventually inherited his title and estate from his paternal uncle and moved to Newstead Abbey, his ancestral home in Nottinghamshire, England. In spite of this legacy, Byron's childhood was often difficult, frequently lonely, and marred by a birth defect. He was born with a club foot, a deformity that made his right foot turn inward so that he walked on its side. He was extremely sensitive about his limp, but found considerable solace in his love for animals, a love that continued throughout his life.

While attending Trinity College, Cambridge University, Byron was dismayed to discover that university rules banned pet dogs. Always resentful of authority, he brought along a pet bear, taking great joy in the realization that there were no rules specifically forbidding bears. He even once suggested that the beast should "sit for a fellowship."

Back home at Newstead Abbey, he also had a number of dogs, including Boatswain, who was born in Newfoundland in May 1803. Byron always described him as a Newfoundland dog, but pictorial evidence suggests Boatswain may have been part husky. Breed standards were not set at the time, so it is highly likely that the dog had mixed ancestry. However, at least one of his ancestors must have been a Newfoundland dog, because Boatswain was an excellent swimmer.

And so was his master. Swimming was one activity that Byron was able to enjoy despite his handicap. According to a tenant farmer, Byron often packed Boatswain and Thunder, another Newfoundland dog, into his boat and rowed to the middle of the lake. Then he would release the oars and jump into the water. Immediately, both the dogs would follow, grab either side of Byron's collar and pull him to shore.

Thunder was larger than Boatswain, but according to one of the family servants, not quite as brave. One of the pastimes that amused Byron was to set his dogs upon his pet bear. Thunder usually shied away from such encounters, but Boatswain apparently faced the larger animal without hesitation.

When Byron travelled, he often brought some of his pets with him. In August 1806, he visited his old school friend

A young boy sits with a St. Bernard–Newfoundland dog for this photo taken in the late 19th century.

Edward Long in Worthing. Henry, Long's younger brother, recalled Byron's arrival with his horses and Boatswain, who was three at the time. Soon after he arrived, Byron decided to do some target practice on the pier, firing his pistol at oyster shells. At one point, Boatswain jumped off the pier and into the river, possibly to chase the shells, but perhaps simply to get some relief from the August heat. It was "a feat," Henry wrote, "which my brother could not prevail upon his dog Fish to perform."

Byron's dogs apparently had considerable freedom and this led to tragedy for Boatswain, who often followed the postboy, or mail carrier, into nearby Mansfield. On one trip, Boatswain was bitten by another dog and contracted rabies.

Byron had no idea that the virus was attacking Boatswain's nervous system until the day the dog had his first seizure. Even then, Byron wiped the foam away from his favourite's mouth with his bare hands—a dangerous action, since the rabies virus can be passed through cuts in the skin. Byron was devastated at the thought of losing his beloved companion, but there was nothing that could be done to save the young Newfoundland dog. On November 18, 1808, Byron wrote to a friend, "Boatswain is dead! He expired in a state of madness on the 10th after suffering much, yet retaining all the gentleness of his nature to the last, never attempting to do the least injury to any one near him."

Byron felt he had lost everyone dear to him except Old Murray, a family servant. Not surprisingly, he expressed his grief in verse. The untitled poem he wrote soon after Boatswain's death includes several lines celebrating the characteristics that make so many people love dogs.

> . . . the poor dog, in life the firmest friend,
> The first to welcome, foremost to defend,
> Whose honest heart is still his master's own,
> Who labours, fights, lives, breathes for him alone.

Other lines criticize the belief that unworthy men have souls, while dogs do not. As far as Byron was concerned, many dogs were more deserving of paradise than men. Byron planned to have a tomb built for Boatswain where Newstead Abbey's church had once been. Instead, the marble tomb was built in the garden and the entire poem inscribed on it. The final two lines read:

> To mark a friend's remains these stones arise;
> I never knew but one,—and here he lies

When Byron first wrote the poem in Boatswain's memory, he showed it to a friend, John Cam Hobhouse. Although Hobhouse thought the whole business rather farcical, he nevertheless humoured Byron by writing his own memorial to Boatswain:

> Near this spot
> Are deposited the Remains of one
> Who possessed Beauty without Vanity,
> Strength without Insolence,
> Courage without Ferocity,
> And all the Virtues of Man without his Vices.
> This Praise, which would be unmeaning Flattery
> If inscribed over human ashes,
> Is but a just tribute to the Memory of
> BOATSWAIN, a Dog.

Boatswain's memorial, which is the only building Byron ever completed at his ancestral home, contains both inscriptions and still stands today.

Byron made sure friends and family knew he wanted to be buried alongside the dog. However, when the poet died in January 1824 after contracting a fever while fighting for Greek independence, his heart was buried in Greece. The remainder of his body was returned to England and buried in the Church of St. Mary Magdalen in Hucknall, not far from Newstead Abbey.

Byron's wishes may not have been fulfilled, but his fame and writing ability have immortalized the affection that sprang up more than 200 years ago between a sensitive, troubled man and a devoted dog.

Jumbo
the Elephant

BRITONS WERE FURIOUS. A NATIONAL treasure was about to be sent to the United States. There were angry discussions on the streets and in parlours, enraged letters to newspapers, prayer vigils and legal action. Although a temporary injunction delayed the final outcome, in the end none of the protests could stand up against US dollars. After paying £2,000 (about Can$10,000 at the time) to the London Zoological Gardens, Phineas T. Barnum, circus owner and consummate showman, became the new owner of Jumbo the elephant.

Jumbo was 21, reputedly the largest elephant in the world and certainly the most famous. He had been captured as a youngster in the French Sudan, south of Lake Chad, in 1861. His first European home was at the Jardin des Plantes in Paris, where he lived with a young female elephant, Alice. Around 1865, however, the two young elephants became ill. Matthew Scott, a British zookeeper, was called in. After examining Jumbo and Alice, Scott concluded that the elephants would probably recover with the care he could provide at London's Zoological Gardens. So he arranged a trade—an African rhinoceros in exchange for the elephants—and Jumbo and Alice moved across the English Channel to settle in at the zoo in Regent's Park. It was a fortunate move for both of them. In 1871, during the Franco-Prussian War, many of the exotic animals at the Jardin des Plantes, including two elephants, Castor and Pollux, were consumed by starving Parisians.

Both Jumbo and Alice thrived under Scott's care. Jumbo quickly became one of the most popular attractions at the zoo, especially with children. He would take food out of their hands with his trunk or carry them in a howdah (a canopied seat) on his back. No trip to the zoo was complete without a long visit with Jumbo, the gentle giant who was probably the most famous animal of the era. Victorians were fascinated by the exotic, both for scientific and political reasons, and Jumbo symbolized both. He was a natural wonder, but was also a reminder of the empire on which the sun never set, an empire that included such extraordinary beasts as elephants and camels.

Jumbo's fame also spread because of the increasing availability of newspapers. Cheaper printing costs, an international telegraph system and higher literacy rates all shaped a new age of information where newspapers were the most important medium. The news they contained wasn't always accurate, and in Jumbo's case it was often overly sentimental. Sometimes, Jumbo was referred to as a "brute" or a "beast," but at other times he was described as almost human. Much was made of his relationship with Alice, the female elephant whom some newspapers described as his "little wife."

Jumbo was a genuine celebrity whose every move attracted attention and admiration. Then, in 1880, Matthew Scott and others at the Regent's Park Zoo became concerned. Although he was still gentle with visitors, Jumbo began showing signs of bad temper. He charged the wall of the elephant house, breaking off a tusk in the process. Zoo officials became worried that Jumbo might misbehave in public and harm someone. When Phineas T. Barnum offered to purchase the mighty beast, it seemed like the best solution to a difficult problem. Arrangements were made to ship the elephant to the United States in March 1882.

Barnum had owned at least 20 elephants by this point and had his own elephant expert, William Newman, a.k.a. "Elephant Bill." Newman was sent to England to oversee Jumbo's passage overseas. Under Newman's supervision, a wheeled wooden crate was placed outside the elephant house. The plan was to move Jumbo into it, close it up and then transport the crate to a waiting ship.

Jumbo the elephant was the largest elephant people had ever seen—in the wild or in captivity.

Moving an 11-foot, 7-ton elephant turned out to be more challenging than anyone had anticipated, even with the assistance of Matthew Scott, whom Jumbo trusted completely. When Newman and Scott tried to confine the elephant's movements to a narrow area between the elephant house and the crate by wrapping chains around his front legs, Jumbo became distressed and tried to break the chains, but the men persisted. They wrapped more chains around his body, then around his head, just above the tusks. When he realized how much his movements were restricted, Jumbo became agitated, trumpeting loudly and trying to break free. Meanwhile, other elephants in the zoo, including Alice, responded to his calls of distress.

Eventually, Jumbo tired of struggling and stood calmly. Scott sat beside him, feeding him biscuits, before trying to coax him into the crate. Jumbo moved forward until he reached the crate, but nothing could induce him to enter the wooden box. Scott and Newman decided to call it a day, and Jumbo was returned to the elephant house.

The next day, the men tried to convince Jumbo to walk to the dock and the waiting ship. He arrived at the gate outside the zoo's parrot house without much difficulty, but between the gate and the road, Jumbo decided to test a patch of ground. According to the London Illustrated News, the big elephant was more accustomed to walking on the gravel that was spread around the zoo. When he strayed off the gravel and onto a patch of earth, Jumbo decided the ground was unsafe and refused to move another step. He moaned sadly, caressed Matthew Scott with his trunk and knelt in front of him. Again, his pitiful cries upset the other elephants. "At the sound of Alice's increasing lamentations, Jumbo became almost frantic, and flung himself down on his side."

The decision to sell Jumbo to Barnum and the methods used to move him sound cruel to us today and are a sad illustration of the lack of knowledge about elephants and wild animals in general. However, most of the people involved in

Jumbo's care were very concerned about his welfare. Circuses and zoos may not have been the ideal location for wild animals, but they did foster curiosity about exotic creatures, and that curiosity eventually led to better understanding and treatment of animals. We may criticize the people of the past for their treatment of animals, but usually they were trying to be humane, at least as they understood it.

In the same way, future generations may criticize late 20th- and early 21st-century zoo staff for their treatment of various animals. Animals are frequently moved to different zoos, sometimes for breeding purposes, sometimes in exchange for different species, sometimes to increase public attendance. Zoo staff do everything in their power to ensure the health and well-being of the animals under their care, yet there is much they still have to learn about animal behaviour. For instance, one study found that elephants in particular are much more likely to die after being transferred to a new zoo, not because of physical harm, but because of the stress of being removed from a familiar social network.

It is clear that Jumbo experienced terrible stress as he was wrenched from his elephant family, but although some 19th-century animal lovers may have had their suspicions about the detrimental effects of moving animals from familiar surroundings, nothing was going to stop Jumbo's transfer to America. It took a few more days, but on Wednesday, March 22, Jumbo was loaded into his packing crate. With his trunk protruding from the front of the box, he was pulled through the streets of London by a team of strong workhorses and then hoisted by a steam-powered crane onto a barge. After a brief trip down the river, the crate was placed on the docks, where it stayed until Friday morning. Then Bill Newman and Matthew Scott climbed onto a little cage in the front of the box. While Newman directed the workmen to minimize the motion of the box, Scott calmed Jumbo by patting his trunk. It took just eight minutes to lift the crate—elephant, trainers and all—into the hold of the *Assyrian Monarch*. When Newman gave the signal that everything was all right, a resounding cheer went up from spectators on the docks and aboard ship.

A number of special guests enjoyed luncheon in the ship's saloon while Jumbo became accustomed to his new temporary quarters. Also on board were supplies for the voyage, including two tons of hay, three sacks of oats, biscuits and a sack of onions—one of Jumbo's favourite treats. In addition to Matthew Scott and Bill Newman, a member of the Society for the Prevention of Cruelty to Animals accompanied the famous elephant on his voyage to the United States. Aside from a little agitation and one bout of seasickness, Jumbo was quite comfortable during the voyage. Scott, Newman and other passengers made a point of visiting him frequently, and Jumbo thoroughly enjoyed the company. He also appreciated the fruit and other special treats visitors brought him, as well as Scotch whisky, which he was given regularly.

Jumbo reached New York on April 10, 1882, and was welcomed with great fanfare. Thousands of New Yorkers turned up to see the most famous animal in the world, and many of them followed Jumbo and his keepers as they paraded through the streets to the Hippodrome building at Madison Square Garden. Soon afterward, he was formally introduced to the other elephants in Barnum and Bailey's Circus. After a performance at Madison Square Garden, 18 elephants were lined up in one of the circus rings. Then Scott slowly led Jumbo down the line. The *New York Tribune* reported:

> One or two of the youngest elephants gave audible evidence of their agitation. They were quickly frowned down by the older ones, and the whole party put on a most dignified and serene appearance. As Jumbo passed along he was greeted with uplifted trunks. He returned the salute and shook trunks with the party in a friendly but rather bored manner.

Jumbo's interest perked up when he encountered Baby, a young female. "It was evidently a case of love at first sight," gushed a reporter from the *Tribune*. Baby was naturally thrown into a flutter of excitement, but she managed to keep up a decent appearance of coyness. She finally consented, however, to shake trunks with her admirer, and after a while allowed herself to be caressed, even going so far as to return her lover's endearments. The other female elephants present were scandalized, and wound their trunks together as if saying, "Oh, the bold-faced thing, did you ever!"

Jumbo spent the next few years touring the United States and Canada, where he proved to be a great favourite. As he had done in England, he continued to take children for rides on his back, both before and after the circus shows. Under the big top, one of the highlights of each performance was the parade of about 30 elephants, with Jumbo in the lead. After the big pachyderms had lined up in the ring, their names were called, and each in turn stepped forward.

As far as Barnum was concerned, animal acts were essential to the success of a circus. In fact, he felt that many people came primarily to see the animals, and if they also happened to catch the performance of high-wire artists or clowns, that was a bonus. In his opinion, Jumbo was worth at least $100,000 to the show. "He did not cost that much by a great deal. But the fact that he is the biggest elephant in the world distinguishes us from all competitors."

What Barnum did not say when he made that statement in the spring of 1884 was that Jumbo was suffering from some undetermined health problems. Realizing how much money he could lose, Barnum made arrangements to have Jumbo's body stuffed if the elephant died suddenly. He also approached London Zoo, asking if he could purchase Alice. Barnum's plan, in the event of Jumbo's demise, was to have Jumbo's "widow" go on tour along with the stuffed skin of her dearly departed.

In the meantime, Barnum was planning a triumphant tour of England, convinced that people would pay handsomely to see Jumbo back on British soil. But first he had to complete the 1885 summer tour. The circus moved along railway lines in the northern United States and southern Canada, usually travelling at night and bringing a touch of exotic entertainment to small Victorian towns during the day.

On September 15, the Barnum and Bailey circus was in St. Thomas, southwest of London, Ontario. Two parallel railway tracks ran close to the grounds where the tents were pitched. Although a level crossing was a short distance away, the circus had received permission from the Grand Trunk Railway to take down some fencing. This way, they could quickly move the animals along the track before and after the shows.

Two performances were scheduled that day, the second one in the evening. By 9 p.m., all of the elephants except Jumbo and Tom Thumb, a small "clown elephant," had been returned to their cages on the circus train. Around 9:30 p.m., Matthew Scott escorted the two animals toward their cages. They were still some distance away when a special freight train appeared in the east.

Realizing the danger, Scott tried to move the elephants down the embankment on the side of the track. When this failed, he urged them to run toward the circus train, where they could get off the main track more easily. Jumbo led the way, with Tom Thumb following close behind. They had gone only 27 metres or so when Tom Thumb was struck from behind and tossed into the ditch, breaking his leg. Seconds later, the locomotive hit Jumbo in the back of the legs, bringing him to his knees. The huge animal cried out in pain as he was hurled into the rear of the circus train. The impact, witnesses said, was like two trains colliding, and the force was great enough to derail the oncoming locomotive and two cars.

Jumbo was mortally wounded. As he lay silently on the tracks, the big elephant reached out and slipped his trunk into Matthew Scott's hand. The man who had been his closest human companion for 14 years did what he could to comfort the creature he loved, but within 15 minutes, Jumbo was dead. The elephant that had entertained Europe and North America for so many years was gone.

In spite of their shock and grief, witnesses then had to deal with practical matters. Jumbo's body was blocking the tracks. Circus members, railway workers and spectators joined together to throw ropes around the giant corpse and roll it out of the way.

The news was telegraphed around the world, setting off waves of public mourning. "Jumbo is dead," announced the *Washington Star*. "The friend of youth, the admired of all, the boast and wonder of the age is no more, and what remains to us is to bear our loss with resignation."

Meanwhile, Phineas T. Barnum characteristically made the most of the tragedy. For three days, as the grisly business of disposing of Jumbo's carcass was carried out, Barnum charged people a nickel apiece to view the elephant's remains.

He also threatened to sue the railway for $100,000, saying that they had been at fault in not warning the circus about the special freight train. The matter was settled out of court, with the Grand Trunk agreeing to provide transportation worth $5,000 to the circus. As it turned out, a crafty lawyer omitted one of the destinations on the circus route, and when Barnum negotiated the travelling costs to that particular town, he was charged $5,000!

Barnum might have been bested in that instance, but his other plans for Jumbo materialized as planned. The famous elephant's body was stuffed, Alice left London for North America, and in 1886 the two elephants toured the United States and Canada together. Then a serious fire broke out in the circus' winter quarters. Although Jumbo's remains were saved, Alice died in the fire.

In 1889, Barnum donated Jumbo's remains to Tufts University in Maryland, where the elephant became the school's mascot. Following a 1975 fire, some of Jumbo's ashes were collected in a peanut butter jar and stored in the university's athletic department. Ten years later, St. Thomas, Ontario, commemorated the 100th anniversary of Jumbo's death with a statue of the popular pachyderm. Designed by Winston Bronnum in Sussex, New Brunswick, the statue was made of concrete and reinforced steel. It was transported by highway to St. Thomas, then unveiled during a five-day festival. The statue still stands today, a reminder of one of the most celebrated animals of the Victorian era.

The Real
Winnie-the-Pooh

ON AUGUST 24, 1914, LIEUTENANT Harry Colebourn stepped off the train in White River, Ontario. Colebourn was a 27-year-old veterinarian with the Fort Garry Horse. Just 20 days earlier, Britain had declared war on Germany, automatically involving Canada in hostilities. Canadians were quick to respond to the call to arms, and among the first men to be mobilized were members of various militia units.

Harry Colebourn was one of these men. At 18 he had emigrated from England to Canada, living first in Toronto, where he graduated from the Ontario Veterinary College in 1911. A short time later, he took a job with the Canadian Department of Agriculture and moved to Winnipeg. Like many young men of the time, Harry joined the local militia, where his duties included caring for cavalry horses.

With a war now underway, Harry had been assigned to watch over the transportation of hundreds of horses to Valcartier, Quebec, the mustering point for Canadian troops. When the train stopped in White River, Ontario, Harry and other soldiers took the opportunity to stretch their legs and get a little fresh air.

As he walked along the station platform, Harry was attracted by an unusual sight. A man was sitting on a bench with a bear cub tied beside him. Ever curious about animals, the young lieutenant walked over and struck up a conversation. In no time at all, he learned that the man was a trapper who had shot a mother bear a few months earlier. Rather than abandon her twin cubs to certain death, he had taken both of them home, but one had subsequently died. The survivor, a seven-month-old female, was standing beside him.

The cub was an American black bear, the most common bear in North America. Compared to grizzlies or polar bears, *Ursus americanus* is on the small side, reaching a height of about 1.5 or 2 metres, and a weight of between 135 and 225 kilograms in adulthood. In some ways similar to dogs, bears have for centuries been adopted as pets or have been trained to perform. Bear cubs, which are especially endearing since they vocalize, beg and play like puppies, have traditionally been prized by many military troops. In fact, Mollie Cope, a white woman adopted by the Mi'kmaq of Nova Scotia in the early 1800s, supported herself by catching cubs and selling them to officers at the Halifax garrison.

Perhaps this military custom occurred to Colebourn as he stood considering the bear. Or perhaps, due to his veterinary sensibilities, he was concerned that the young cub might suffer her sibling's fate. But there was also something about the little bear that was uniquely appealing, and it did not take Colebourn long to reach a decision. Before the train pulled out of the station, he paid the trapper $20. It was a significant amount, equivalent to about $350 in 2006, and more than many men earned in a week. The young female was promptly dubbed Winnipeg Bear, which was quickly shortened to Winnie. By the time Harry, the horses and other soldiers reached Valcartier, Winnie had become the darling of the regiment.

The stay in Quebec was brief. On September 28, Harry Colebourn and his brothers-in-arms sailed for England aboard the S.S. *Manitou*, bringing Winnie along with them. After they docked in Devonport on October 17, they moved to Salisbury, where soldiers from Britain, Canada and other Commonwealth countries were gathering prior to being sent to the continent.

It was a typical military situation: "Hurry up and wait." Although some of the soldiers were undoubtedly impressed by Stonehenge, many were impatient, irritated and disgruntled. Aside from dealing with the frustrations of

Harry Colebourn helps Winnie drink from a bottle in Salisbury Plain, England, in 1914.

military life, the men had to cope with camping out through one of the coldest, wettest autumns in years. There was mud everywhere, making it almost impossible to keep themselves clean or comfortable. And, of course, there was the constant anxiety about what awaited them on the front.

Winnie provided welcome relief. Under Harry Colebourn's tender care, she grew taller and heavier. She was so docile that she would allow anyone to take her food away from her, and much of the time she followed the soldiers around, just as a dog would. At night, she slept under Harry's cot in his tent. Harry taught her a number of tricks, most based on her natural abilities, such as begging and tree climbing. At first, Winnie enjoyed climbing the central pole in the tent and shaking it a few times, but as she put on weight there were concerns that she would shake the pole loose and collapse the tent. So a tree trunk was positioned outside for her enjoyment.

Although there were many who believed the war would be over by Christmas, there was still a sense of the historic importance of the times. Many photographs were taken of the soldiers, both individual pictures and group shots, and Winnie was included in a number of them.

Winnie was not the only Canadian bear in England. There were at least five others brought over by soldiers. While their presence was accepted as long as the troops were awaiting orders, there was no question of the animals being allowed to accompany the Canadian contingent into battle. In early December, Harry was notified that he must make provisions for Winnie's care. On December 9, he borrowed a car, tucked Winnie inside and sped off to London.

As a veterinarian and a great lover of animals, Harry was certainly aware of the reputation of London Zoo, which had been collecting exotic animals since 1828. One of the newest innovations at the zoo was Mappin's Terraces, named for the jewellery company that had funded the project. Completed earlier in 1914, the terraces were designed for bears and other animals and featured concrete mountains and caves. It seemed a perfect temporary home for Winnie while Harry was across the Channel, and soon matters were arranged. Winnipeg Bear was loaned to London Zoo for the duration of the war.

Winnie was still a cub, not quite a year old, when she was installed in Mappin's Terraces. Her first companion was a Himalayan brown bear. Not thrilled to be sharing accommodations with a newcomer, it behaved aggressively. Winnie, sweet-tempered as always, refused to fight with the other animal. After a few tense days, the Himalayan relaxed and they came to some kind of ursine agreement.

For a gregarious creature like Winnie, the zoo was a perfect home. Thousands of visitors came to the zoo each year, many of them children, and Winnie soon won their hearts. She loved the treats she was given, especially the sweet mixture of syrup and condensed milk she drank from a quart-sized bucket held in all four paws. Frequently, when she was finished, she would rock back and forth on her back to show her pleasure. She would also "do her daily dozen" at her keeper's command, lying belly up and moving her legs back and forth as if doing calisthenics.

Because she was so tame, certain visitors were allowed to enter her cage and meet her in close quarters. One visitor described how Winnie would approach people in much the same way as a large dog would, rubbing her flanks against the visitors' legs. Winnie enjoyed company because people often brought her treats, something she greatly appreciated. If anyone showed up at her cage with a brown paper bag, she immediately assumed it contained some goodies and snatched it away as quickly as she could. The *London Daily Express* called her "Winsome Winnie, the dearest, tamest, most affectionate bear in the United Kingdom."

The war that was supposed to be over by Christmas raged on for more than four bloody years. Harry Colebourn occasionally returned to England on leave and often visited Winnie at London Zoo. He fully intended to take her back with him when the war was over, but sometime in 1919 he changed his mind. Perhaps it was the realization that she was so happy in the zoo. Or perhaps he worried that he couldn't care for her adequately back home in Winnipeg. At any rate, on December 1, 1919, he officially donated Winnie to the zoo. The following year, Harry returned to Canada.

Winnie stayed on in London, continuing to entertain visitors, including a four-year-old boy named Christopher Milne. Christopher was the son of a well-known writer, Alan A. Milne, and in 1924 was allowed to visit Winnie in her cage and cuddle her. Christopher was very fond of a teddy bear he had been given as an infant, and although the toy had had a series of names, the boy decided it would be renamed after his real live bear friend, Winnie. "Pooh" was tacked on in honour of a pet swan he had once known.

Winnie-the-Pooh soon became a character in the bedtime

stories A.A. Milne told his son. Just before Christmas 1925, Milne was asked to write a children's story for a London newspaper. At his wife's suggestion, he recounted the adventures of Christopher Robin and Winnie-the-Pooh, the "bear of little brain." Thousands of readers saw the story in the Christmas Eve edition of the newspaper, and thousands more heard the story read on the radio the following day. Winnie-the-Pooh immediately captured the hearts of the public, just as his real-life counterpart had done. The following year, having created a cast of other characters, including Piglet, Tigger and Eeyore, Milne published a book entitled *Winnie-the-Pooh*.

Over the next several years, the adventures of Winnie-the-Pooh were read by millions of children and adults around the world. Meanwhile, the real Winnie continued to entertain visitors in her enclosure at the zoo, although she was now growing old. Her fur still looked smooth and glossy, but she had lost all her teeth and was nearly blind from cataracts in both eyes. She also suffered from arthritis, but remained just as sweet and even-tempered as she had always been. In 1931, zoo officials retired her, taking her off public display, although some visitors were still allowed to call into her private apartment. Finally, Winnie suffered a stroke, and on May 12, 1934, she was put to sleep. The bear that inspired one of the most popular ursine characters of all time would now live only on the pages of Milne's books.

As the fictional Winnie continued to gain popularity,

Harry and Winnie pose in Valcartier in August 1914.

people forgot about the real black bear from Winnipeg. After Disney acquired rights to the character in the 1960s, the lovely drawings created by artist F.H. Shephard for A.A. Milne's book morphed into the cuddly Disney cartoon character. Few people had any idea that the beloved, honey-loving cartoon bear had any connection to Canada.

Then, in 1987, a Calgary newspaper told the story of the bear who had inspired the fictional character and claimed that a regiment other than the Fort Garry Horse had donated the bear to the zoo. Harry Colebourn had died 40 years earlier, but his son, Fred, saw the story and decided to set the record straight. The subsequent publicity revived interest in Winnie in Canada.

White River, the town where Harry and Winnie met, recognized the tourism potential in being known as the home of Winnie-the-Pooh. In 1989, to commemorate the 75th anniversary of Harry Colebourn's meeting with Winnie, townsfolk decided to erect a statue of the cartoon bear. The Disney Corporation objected at first, but gave in after considerable protest and a letter-writing campaign. In 1992, White River installed a 7.5-metre statue of Winnie-the-Pooh on the Trans-Canada Highway, near the entrance to town. The White River statue is instantly recognizable as the lovable cartoon character with his red shirt and ever-present pot of honey.

Canadians have commemorated the real Winnie in other ways. In 1996, Canada Post issued a stamp showing

Harry Colebourn feeding the young bear. And an early photograph of the pair inspired another statue, this one in Winnipeg's Assiniboine Park Zoo. The nearly life-sized bronze by sculptor William Epp shows soldier and cub face to face, looking fondly at one another. It's a poignant moment—seemingly fictional to anyone who does not know their story. For those who do, the sculpture perfectly captures that long-ago time when, in the midst of "the war to end all wars," one very special bear cub touched the hearts of thousands.

CHAPTER

5

Art and Animals: Emily Carr's Menagerie

EMILY CARR IS WIDELY RECOGNIZED as one of Canada's most talented artists. Her favourite subjects were the forests of British Columbia and Native scenes, including totem poles. As a mature artist, her bold colours and impressionistic style won her considerable celebrity. By the time she died in 1945 at the age of 73, she was famous for her outstanding work.

Conventional society often sees artists as odd, eccentric or not quite respectable. This was especially true in the late 19th and early 20th centuries, and doubly so if the artist happened to be a woman. Fortunately, Emily had some advantages. She was raised in a respectable and financially comfortable middle-class home, along with a brother and five older sisters. But she was something of a misfit from an early age, never completely happy with her family's rather rigid views of the world.

As a young girl in Victoria, British Columbia, Emily was a tomboy, happiest when outdoors, especially if animals were involved. She loved birds and during her childhood had a crow, a peacock and several ducklings as pets, along with a number of dogs and other animals.

Emily's parents died when she was still in her early teens, so her older sisters raised her to adulthood. Like many artistically talented young women of the 1890s, she began teaching art to children. In 1899, she travelled to England to further her education, but a mental and physical collapse sent her to a Suffolk sanatorium in 1902. There she became so fascinated by English songbirds that she began raising them, stealing the young birds from their nests before they opened their eyes. This way, they would imprint on her, becoming as attached to her as they normally would to their parents. Soon other patients and members of the hospital staff were helping out by finding worms to feed Emily's feathered friends. When her illness intervened and she was no longer able to care for the birds, Emily had them humanely destroyed.

Back in Victoria in 1904, Emily began making painting trips to the northern part of Vancouver Island. She was fascinated by the Native people in that area, as well as by their art and the forest that surrounded them. Often she travelled on horseback, usually accompanied by a dog or two. Then, just before she moved to Vancouver in 1906, a very special dog entered her life.

Billie was a mongrel, part bobtailed sheep dog. Emily wrote that she had little admiration for Billie's other half, but claimed his bobtail half "was crammed with the loyalty, loveableness, wisdom, courage and kindness of the breed." Yet, when someone first offered him to her as a pet, she was not keen on the arrangement. He was already three and had bitten people several times. Still, Emily found animals nearly impossible to resist, and against her better judgment she adopted Billie. He remained Emily's close companion for 13 years.

Emily's reluctance to accept Billie was somewhat out of character because she was forever acquiring new pets, including some rather strange animals. In 1908, she was on a trip to Buccaneer Bay to visit some friends when she bought a baby vulture from some Native people. Uncle Tom, who cost 50 cents, slept on the floor of Emily's tent along with Billie and a pet cockatoo. When Emily went out to sketch, the cockatoo perched on her shoulder, while Billie and Uncle Tom trotted along on either side of her.

Feeding Uncle Tom posed some problems, but Emily solved them by digging clams and mussels for him. "He grew into a great bird," she later reported, "but he would not accept his freedom. I donated him to Stanley Park and when I used to go to see him he ran to me rejoicing."

By 1913, Emily Carr had created a substantial body of

work, although she often destroyed paintings she considered unsatisfactory. She was slowly becoming recognized, but was still unable to earn enough from her art to support herself. Now in her early forties, Emily took her inheritance and built a house with four apartments on the Carr family property in Victoria. One of the apartments would serve as her home and studio. The other three she rented to boarders.

But Emily Carr was not cut out to be a boarding-house landlady. She was rather eccentric, difficult to get along with and was frequently suspicious that people were criticizing her or lying to her. Nevertheless, she ran the boarding house for 15 years. And, in between cooking and cleaning and otherwise tending to the needs of her boarders, she established a dog kennel.

The idea had been growing for years, but what finally made up Emily's mind was Billie's death. Bobtailed sheep dogs were still in short supply in Canada, although they were highly valued for herding sheep and cattle. With considerable difficulty, Emily found the right dogs to start her kennel.

In many ways, the project was quite successful. Emily loved the dogs. To feed them, she bought meat at the public market and packed some into the old wicker baby buggy she used for carrying clay or other items. Then she loaded the rest of the meat into packs, put them on the backs of some of the older dogs, and together they headed back to the boarding house. There she turned the meat into stew for her bobtails. When she fed the dogs, she sang to them,

Billie the dog, Sallie the cockatoo and Jane the parrot sit for a photo.

working each dog's name into little nonsense verses to get their attention.

Emily's dogs were highly regarded, but running the kennel was hard work. Usually, she would not let any of the females raise litters of more than six pups, but if there was a great demand for the dogs, she would bend her rule. To make sure every pup was as well nourished as possible, she bottle-fed them. One summer, with 30 pups in the kennel, she spent three hours a day for three weeks on feedings alone.

In four years, Emily raised and sold 350 pups. But there were heartbreaks along the way. When distemper broke out in the kennel, she had to destroy several animals. And, although the kennel was supposed to be a paying enterprise, Emily sometimes refused to sell a dog if she did not like the look of the customer. Eventually, the business was costing too much money, and after she sold some property in 1921, there was simply not enough room to continue raising large dogs. Emily sold all of her bobtails except one. The decision gave her more free time but came with a high psychological price. "Emptying the kennel was numbness," she later wrote.

Some of the tenants were probably relieved, but they still had to contend with Emily's menagerie of other pets. Aside from a white rat or two, which were usually caged, she had Jane, a talking yellow-and-green Panama parrot; Adolphs, a silver grey Persian cat; and Ginger Pop, a Belgian Griffon dog, plus various hens, rabbits and birds. During the year

Emily Carr on a picnic with her old Billie dog.

she closed the kennel, Emily adopted her most exotic and entertaining pet, Woo.

Emily acquired this Javanese monkey plus $35 in exchange for a bobtail pup. At night, Woo slept in the basement, but during the day she stayed at Emily's side, or at least in the studio. Typically, the monkey wore a collar, which was attached to a chain. When Emily ate with her boarders, Woo was usually chained to one end of the table, where she occasionally helped herself to food.

In spite of her family and professional connections, Emily was a very lonely woman, frequently distrustful of other people and their motives. But she understood and trusted animals and had an affectionate heart. In many ways the little monkey became a surrogate child. Before putting Woo into the cage at night, Emily usually recited "This little piggie went to market" to her and then sang lullabies until her pet fell asleep in her arms.

One thing Emily insisted upon was that Woo wear dresses, which Emily either sewed or knitted herself. At first, Woo resisted the unfamiliar clothing, but Emily was as strong-willed as her pet and sewed up the back of the garment to stop her from removing it. Woo fidgeted and tore at the clothing, but when she calmed down, Emily put a little treat in the front pocket of her dress. It took a few attempts before Woo understood what was going on—and before she learned to retrieve her treats without tearing the pocket—but eventually the monkey adapted to the dresses.

The collar was another matter. Sometimes it was placed around Woo's neck, sometimes around her waist. It really did not matter, since the monkey's nimble fingers were perfectly capable of undoing the buckle. Carol Pearson, Emily's student and surrogate daughter, recalled how she and Emily used to leave Woo behind in the studio and then spy on her. If she decided to remove her collar, Woo would carefully fasten it before putting it down on the floor. Then she would wander about the room, seeing what kind of mischief she could get into.

The monkey would glance over one shoulder, then the other, obviously feeling very guilty. "Ooo, OOOHH ooOOO," she would mutter, her little lips pursed, for all the world like a naughty child about to raid the cookie jar and wondering how much time remained before Mama returned.

In fact, Woo often did behave like a naughty child. If the remnants of a tea party were left behind, Woo would investigate, draining each cup in turn, scooping out whatever sugar might be left and gently replacing the cup in its saucer—upside down. Other times, she might go in search of sunflower seeds, stuff as many into her cheeks as she could and climb up to the two birds that Emily kept together in a cage. Woo might feed some sunflowers to the birds, but she was just as likely to shake their cage and make them shriek.

Sometimes Woo's antics were a little more serious, and if Emily and Carol thought she was going to get into real trouble when they were spying on her, one of them would rattle the doorknob. Woo's immediate reaction was to rush back to her collar, fasten it on, turn her back to the direction from which the sound had come and sit quietly, fiddling with her dress as though nothing had happened. Emily and Carol learned from secretly watching Woo, as well as from experience, that if she greeted them excitedly when they returned from an outing, she had probably been very well behaved. If she was subdued and ignored them, she had almost certainly been up to no good.

One of her favourite pranks involved Jane, the parrot. If the animals were home alone and the telephone rang, Woo would pick up the receiver and hold it close to Jane. "Hello, hello!" the parrot would squawk. Typically, the caller would ask for Emily.

"And who else?" Jane would respond. Once she got her answer, she would usually order, "Speak up! Speak up!"

If the caller had no idea what was going on, this would continue for some time. The caller became more confused, the parrot more excited. Finally, as Jane shrieked with all her might, Woo would develop the simian equivalent of a guilty conscience and hurriedly hang up the phone.

Jane wasn't the only pet to bear the brunt of Woo's escapades. Woo and CoCo, one of the Griffons, were often chained together—but not leashed—when Emily and Carol went for walks. It took a little while for the monkey and the dog to work out a comfortable routine. CoCo was stronger than Woo, and if he stopped suddenly, Woo felt a terrific tug on her collar. She eventually learned that if she walked along holding a few links of the chain in her paw, she had enough slack to compensate for any sudden stops. However, the little monkey lacked the strength to keep the dog still long enough for her to satisfy her curiosity about things she encountered on the walks. She solved that problem by stuffing part of the chain in the cracks of the wooden sidewalk. This effectively held CoCo in place until Woo was ready to move along. The monkey took great delight in waiting until Emily and Carol were nearly out of sight and CoCo was frantic about the possibility of being left behind. Then Woo would quickly release the chain, leap onto CoCo's back and hang on tightly as the dog ran full speed to catch up.

Woo enjoyed teasing CoCo, but apparently felt some affection toward him. If CoCo tangled up his chain and Woo saw that Emily or Carol was aware of it, she would jump up and down and mock the dog. But if the humans seemed oblivious to the dog's predicament, Woo would quietly untangle her canine companion.

Like most monkeys, Woo was a great mimic, and she often used her gift to get attention. Visitors who called on Emily fussed over Woo, at least for a little while. However, if Woo felt she was being neglected, she often picked out a magazine, one of the smaller formats which were easier for her little hands to manage. Then she would carefully turn over the pages, looking up at the guest every few seconds. When she finally caught the person's eye, she would quickly close the magazine, but keep one finger inside. Then she would wrap her arms about her body and rock back and forth, as if laughing. Few people could resist Woo's antics, and this encouraged her to carry on even more. Usually, all eyes focused on her, even those of the three Belgian Griffons Emily kept in the studio.

But Woo's talent for mimicry sometimes got her into trouble. Once, when Emily and her student were out for one of their long walks together, Carol picked up a plant that turned out to be poisonous. When she developed an itchy

Emily Carr feeds her pets: Woo the monkey (on Carr's right shoulder), her dogs CoCo and Ginger Pop, and Adolphus the cat.

rash on her hands and on one side of her face, Emily gave her a tube of yellow ointment. The medicine worked, but had some unforeseen consequences. Returning from an outing one day, Emily and Carol found Woo's face and hands covered with green paint. She had seen what Carol did after squeezing what looked like a paint tube and decided to try it for herself.

Woo once took her interest in Emily's paints too far. She became extremely sick after eating a tube of yellow paint. Emily used every treatment she could think of, wiping the monkey's mouth and throat with gasoline-soaked rags and giving her medicine to make her vomit. But Woo spat out the medicine. Then Emily filled a hot water bottle, placed it on her lap and laid Woo on top of it.

To make matters even more stressful, Emily was scheduled to speak at the prestigious Women's Canadian Club in Victoria the following day, March 4, 1930. Arrangements had been made for an exhibition of her works as part of the lecture, and although she was not particularly keen about public appearances, Emily realized how important this event was. Fortunately, Woo recovered quickly and Emily prepared to go to the Women's Canadian Club.

For moral support she brought along Ginger Pop, one of her Belgian Griffons. It was a good thing she did. Already upset about Woo's mishap, Emily was extremely nervous in front of the audience of 500 people. She was trembling as she began and was so nervous that her voice could barely be heard. The audience called for her to speak louder, flustering Emily even further.

At that moment, Ginger Pop, who was sitting on the lap of the club president, jumped down, ran over to Emily and sat at her feet. Both the audience and the artist relaxed. Ginger Pop stayed in front of Emily, staring raptly into her face until she successfully finished her speech.

Emily Carr adored her animals, but old age and illness eventually forced her to part with most of them. In 1937, after a serious heart attack, she asked a friend to give most of her pets away before she returned home from the hospital.

She simply could not handle it herself and reasoned that her absence might convince her pets she was gone for good. "If they found out I had not gone but was just hiding, I could not face . . . to send them off," she later wrote. Woo was sent to the monkey house in Stanley Park, and all the dogs but one were given away. By 1944, Emily's menagerie was down to two pets—a budgie and a chipmunk.

Emily Carr died in 1945 and is far better remembered for her magnificent works of art than for her pets. However, she immortalized a number of her animal companions in paintings, sketches and words, leaving behind an enchanting record of her pets' endearing antics and affection.

CHAPTER

Grey Owl and the Beaver People

WHEN ARCHIBALD BELANEY WAS A boy growing up in England, he was fascinated by tales of native North Americans. At 17, he moved to Canada, where he became a hunter, a trapper and an accomplished woodsman. He lived among the Native people, learning their culture and skills, and was eventually adopted by the Ojibway. He also assumed the name Wa-Sha-Quon-Asin, or Grey Owl, although a number of people continued to call him Archie. With only a few hiatuses, including a stint in the army during the first World War, Archie Belaney spent the rest of his life in the Canadian wilderness.

Like many Native people, especially those living in the Canadian north, Archie depended on the wilderness for his survival. Fish and game supplied food for his table;

fur-bearing animals, including beaver, mink and otter, provided pelts that could be sold for much-needed cash. It was a difficult way of life, requiring stamina and skill, but it was one he loved.

In the winter of 1925–26, Archie and an Iroquois woman, Gertrude Bernard, began living together and in the summer of 1926 were married by a Native elder. Gertrude, who was also known as Anahareo, or Pony, had little experience as a trapper—she came from a family of prospectors. However, Anahareo could hunt, and because she was determined to share her husband's way of life, she learned to trap. But she was frequently upset about the pain the animals suffered.

In the spring of 1928, Archie was trapping beavers near Forsyth, Quebec, and began tracking a pair of the animals. It was later in the season than usual, and he knew that the beavers' kittens would have been born. To trap the adults and let the young go free would have caused even more suffering, so he decided to trap the entire family. He and Anahareo went out to find them and saw the kits swimming around. Unable to bear the thought of killing them, Anahareo persuaded Archie to adopt the kittens instead. Archie, who was already suffering some twinges of conscience about killing beavers, agreed. It took a bit of doing, but eventually they loaded the two small animals into their canoe. They were, Archie later wrote, "Two funny-looking furry creatures with little scaly tails and exaggerated hind feet, that weighed less than half a pound apiece, and that tramped sedately up and down the bottom of the canoe, with that steady, persistent, purposeful walk that we were later to know so well."

The kittens were completely unafraid of humans and soon became quite demanding. "Before long they had us trained to sleep with one eye open and one hand on the milk can," Archie remembered. They fed the kittens tinned condensed milk, diluted with a little water. When the kits would not drink from a dish and there was no bottle available, Archie dipped a twig into the sweet milk, put the twig into a young beaver's mouth, closed its mouth over the stick, and pulled on it gently. Not only did the kits swallow the milk, the two also chewed on the twig, which kept them quiet for a little while.

Archie and Anahareo gave the beaver kittens a number of names before settling on McGinnis for the male and McGinty for the female. Collectively, they were referred to as "the Macs." Like a human baby or young cat or dog, the beaver kittens needed more than food. They also liked to be picked up and cuddled, and this became part of a regular routine. First the beavers would eat, then they would crawl up Archie's or Anahareo's sleeve, or, more often, drape themselves across their human friends' necks and fall asleep. If the kittens were moved, they would rouse and then crawl sleepily back to their preferred sleeping spot. There was no question of putting them in their box, where they spent part of their time, because when they wanted attention they would cry out until they got it.

Their vocalizations amazed Archie and Anahareo. Archie wrote:

> Their voices were really the most remarkable thing about them, much resembling the cries of a human infant, without the volume but with a greater variety of expression, and at all hours of the day and night there was liable to be some kind of a new sound issuing from the interior of the box. The best known and easiest to recognize of these was the loud, long and very insistent call for lunch, which chorus broke out about every two hours.

The Macs also responded to human voices and to each other. For little beavers, Archie's tent was a huge territory begging to be explored. But if the kittens were separated for too long, they would cry out and follow the sound until they were reunited. Then they would "throw themselves on their backs with wiggles and squeals of joy, and lie down together holding tightly on to each other's fur." Instinctively, the Macs relied on each other for comfort, but they soon included Archie and Anahareo in their family circle. Each beaver had a favourite person, the female preferring Anahareo, the male preferring Archie. If the kits became anxious or frightened, they would crawl to their favourite and cuddle close until they were comfortable once more.

As the kits grew, they wandered farther and farther from the camp. At first, Archie and Anahareo worried when they

Grey Owl feeds a baby beaver in Riding Mountain National Park, Manitoba.

disappeared, but it soon became apparent that the young beavers would come when called. The humans became overconfident, however, and panicked when McGinnis and McGinty disappeared one day. For 30 hours, Archie and Anahareo hunted everywhere, with no results. Convinced that the kits had been taken by birds of prey, the couple returned sadly to their tent, where they found the two Macs on their blankets, squeezing water out of their fur. After that, Archie and Anahareo pitched their tent closer to the water, kept a sharp watch for predatory birds and let the Macs come and go as they pleased.

By the time they were three months old, the Macs were

more or less independent and were able to find their way around the camp easily. Porridge had replaced milk as their main diet, and they still relied on their human companions for a daily feeding. Although this was an added responsibility for Archie and Anahareo, they found the chore amusing. Once they were finished eating, the two kits would push their plates as far out of the way as possible. From years of observation, Archie knew that beavers kept their lodges very clean, pushing sticks out of the way to maximize their living space. The kits instinctively not only shoved their dinner plates to the walls of the tent, they also tried to stand them on end, in order to free up more space.

Archie and Anahareo also discovered that the beaver kits were very affectionate. They loved to nibble on eyebrows or hair, a bit of fringe or a button. Upon returning from a swim, they would climb onto the blankets covering their sleeping humans, expecting to be greeted warmly, regardless of the time of night. Archie enjoyed their antics, despite his feeling that it was somehow inappropriate to become so emotionally involved with two wild animals.

A strong believer in gendered stereotypes, Archie was not surprised about Anahareo's feelings for the young beavers. But he was perplexed about his own attachment to them, and wrote:

> I wondered at times if it was quite manly to feel as
> I did toward these small beasts. But I was able to

call to my rescue the recollection of an ugly pock-marked Indian, a huge, evil appearing man I had always disliked, but who spent a whole day in the rain searching for a young beaver he had lost; and when he recovered it, he came home in the pouring rain in his shirt sleeves carrying the shivering little creature wrapped up in his coat. Another had killed a good lead-dog for killing a pet beaver he had had for 2 years.

In the fall, when McGinnis and McGinty were about six months old, Archie and Anahareo travelled to a railway town to procure supplies and catch up on news from other trappers. The beaver kittens travelled loose in the canoe and were then placed in a sack for portages.

The tame beaver kittens caused quite a stir, and more than one person offered to buy them from Archie and Anahareo. But the couple found that their new admiration for beavers made the offers unthinkable. Around the same time, they were troubled to learn of two other captive kits that had died, probably from malnutrition.

That fall, Archie spent a lot of time thinking about beavers. The close relationship he had developed with the kits brought back memories of other beavers he had encountered as a trapper. He remembered finding a mother beaver caught by one leg in a trap but still nursing a kit. When she was freed, although she was in great pain, she would not hurry away from the trapper, but waited for her kit to return.

Archie found another beaver hanging by one arm from a spring pole trap. She had been there some time, was near death and was crying in agony. When he cut her down, she grasped one of his fingers tightly with one paw as she died.

Having seen the Macs cling to each other, to himself and to Anahareo when frightened or in need of comfort, Archie realized that beavers were not merely dumb animals. "They seemed to be almost like little folk from some other planet, whose language we could not yet quite understand. To kill such creatures seemed monstrous."

Archie's growing love for the beavers opened his eyes to the animals' plight. In Canada, the wild beaver population was dwindling. High fur prices had brought in many amateurs, and the animals were being overhunted. To make matters worse, many amateurs trapped adult beavers in the spring, before the kits were able to survive on their own. Thanks to his extensive reading, Archie knew about the near-extinction of buffalo on the North American prairies half a century earlier. He also knew that efforts to restore the buffalo herds had met with considerable success. And he began to think about helping the beavers in a similar fashion.

Archie decided he would start a one-man crusade to preserve the Canadian beaver. First, he would locate a family in a place where no one was trapping. Then he would protect it from everyone else, no matter what the cost.

After asking around, Archie, Anahareo and the Macs set out for the Lake Témiscouata area, southeast of

Rivière-de-Loup, and not far from the Quebec–New Brunswick border. It was not the pristine wilderness he had envisioned, but the French-Canadians he encountered were friendly enough.

Unfortunately, the Macs had recently begun to lose their hair. Archie took them to a local doctor, who recommended a change in diet from porridge to a prepared baby food and also provided a salve. The doctor waived his fee, but there was still the food to pay for. Archie had only 30 cents to his name. When the bill for the baby food came to 75 cents, Archie asked the local storekeeper if he could charge it—then boldly asked if he could also charge winter supplies. To his surprise, the storekeeper, already fascinated by the Macs, agreed.

The diet treatment worked, but the trek to the family's new home would bring additional trials. Before the Macs had fully recuperated from their bout of hair loss, they almost drowned in a canoe mishap. Once they were safely recovered, Anahareo bundled them against the cold and kept them close to a warm fire until they resumed their journey.

They walked for days to reach their winter campsite. At each stop along the way, the Macs busied themselves finding bedding or harvesting small saplings. Often, all four individuals—Archie, Anahareo and the two beavers—were busy at the same time. "On more than one occasion one of us had to stand waiting with perhaps an armful of wood, or a pail of water, while some busy little beast manoeuvered for position with a stick in front of the door."

They settled at Birch Lake, where the first order of business was to build a log cabin for the winter. Once the structure was up, Archie prepared to chink the logs with moss. He cut some large pieces of frozen moss then placed them in a semicircle around the stove to thaw overnight. When he and Anahareo woke the next morning, they discovered that the two Macs had been busy chinking the cabin themselves. They may not have been as discriminating as humans—they filled the bottom of the door as well as the walls—but their instincts were sound. In their own lodges, beavers fill every crack that might let in drafts or water, and the two Macs were simply doing what came naturally.

Archie and Anahareo were endlessly amused by their pets' antics at the new cabin. The two kits sometimes quarrelled, especially over food, and would sit as far apart as they could from each other, grumbling warnings under their breath. Sometimes one would tease the other until its sibling shrieked, and then the instigator would shake as though laughing at the fun. They built a kind of den underneath Archie and Anahareo's bed, blocking off the sides with whatever they could find around the cabin and digging a tunnel under the exterior wall. All kinds of items disappeared into the den, for the beavers were extremely curious and stole anything that intrigued them.

That curiosity got McGinty into serious trouble when she picked up some tobacco and ate it. In the middle of the night, she awoke in agony, partially paralyzed from nicotine poisoning. Archie put her on the bunk, where she held tightly to Anahareo's clothes. Archie prepared an emetic, hoping to clear her system, but before McGinty could swallow it, she slipped into a coma. What saved her was the fact that Archie remembered a treatment for opium poisoning. Throughout the night, he and Anahareo took turns rubbing the young beaver in an attempt to keep her awake, then plunging her into successive hot mustard baths. For 10 hours they worked on her, and although her heartbeat seemed to improve, at dawn she suddenly stood up, convulsed and then went rigid.

Archie turned away, unwilling to watch the death of the young creature he had come to love. He later wrote:

> I didn't want to see. There would be a heart break in the death of this small dumb beast. Then I heard a cry behind me, not a wailing, not a lamentation as I had expected, but a declaiming, a discoursing with strange half-human sounds in it, a long loud mono- logue as of one laying down the law.

He turned to see McGinty sitting upright, chattering away while trying to comb mustardy bath water from her coat.

Anahareo was in tears, and McGinnis was equally emo- tional. All through the night he had tried to climb onto the bunk to get close to McGinty. Now that she had recovered, he was able to approach his sister. He smelled her, plucked at her fur with his front paws and as Archie later recalled, "made small sounds, short mumbling little whimpers that we had never heard before." The kits touched noses, then scurried into their den under the bunk. When Archie and Anahareo peeped in, "they were lying with their hands embedded in each other's fur, as they had done when small."

Archie's plans to restore the beaver population failed after the beaver family he had found at the lake was killed by trappers. And in the spring, the Macs suddenly disappeared. Archie and Anahareo searched far and wide, asking anyone who might know of their whereabouts. The young beavers were already well known in the community, but no one was able to discover what had happened to them. Archie and Anahareo were devastated by the loss, although for months afterward they kept hoping the Macs would reappear.

A short time after McGinnis and McGinty vanished, Archie and Anahareo acquired another pair of young beaver kittens. The male died, and for a time it seemed the female would succumb too, but she survived and was named Jelly Roll. Like the Macs, she had her own distinctive personality. Although never as physically affectionate as the other two, Jelly Roll became a celebrity in her own right, sometimes appearing with Archie when he lectured on his life in the wild and the need to preserve the wilderness.

For a time, while Anahareo was prospecting in the Canadian north, Archie and Jelly Roll lived alone together. Then, fearing that she might fall victim to a "marauding otter" that was preying on other beavers, Archie set a trap.

One morning when he went to check the trap he found a male beaver had been caught in it and had dragged it into the lake in his efforts to escape. Archie hauled up the trap and found the beaver barely alive.

> He had a piece of his scalp hanging loose, and half-drowned and scared almost to death, he made little attempt to defend himself. I removed the trap and took him home with me, tied up in a gunny sack. His foot was badly injured, and being one of the all-important hind, or swimming feet, I decided to try and repair the damage before I liberated him.

The male beaver became a permanent member of the household. Archie called him Rawhide after he removed the bit of loose scalp, leaving a patch of raw skin.

Eventually, the beavers' activities came to the attention of the National Parks Service staff, who offered Archie a job at Riding Mountain Park in Manitoba. After some consideration, he accepted—on the condition that he could keep Jelly Roll and Rawhide with him, and that, should the Macs ever show up, he could keep them as well.

In June 1931, soon after Archie relocated to Riding Mountain, the National Parks Service sent cameraman Bill Oliver to film him. The documentary *The Beaver People* showed Jelly Roll and Rawhide swimming, diving, hauling sticks and climbing in and out of Archie's canoe. The film also accomplished the Parks Service's main goal: boosting awareness of the national park system and attracting tourists to Riding Mountain to meet Grey Owl and his tame beavers.

Archie and Anahareo, who both continued to promote conservation efforts through lectures, film and writing, probably saved hundreds—if not thousands—of beavers from cruel deaths. But it was the Macs, Jelly Roll and Rawhide who captured the public imagination. As Archie observed, beavers seemed like small alien people, rather than animals. Describing Jelly Roll, he wrote,

> A dog, for all his affection and fidelity, had little power of self-expression, and his activities differed greatly from those of a human being; a dog was sometimes too utterly submissive. This creature comported itself as a person, of a kind, and she busied herself at tasks that I could, without loss of dignity, have occupied myself at; she made camp, procured and carried in supplies, could lay plans and carry them out and stood robustly and resolutely on her own hind legs, metaphorically and actually, and had an independence of spirit that measured up well with my own, seeming to look on me as a contemporary, accepting me as an equal and no more.

7

Prime Minister King's "Little Angel Dogs"

IN 1944, CANADIAN PRIME MINISTER William Lyon Mackenzie King celebrated his 25th anniversary as leader of the federal Liberal party. A congratulatory banquet was held at Ottawa's Château Laurier Hotel on August 7, 1944. There were many speeches praising King's leadership and accomplishments, as well as the presentation of some tokens of appreciation. Among the latter was a silver statuette depicting the prime minister and his late pet dog, Pat.

King acknowledged the statuette by paying tribute to his "little friend Pat" in a speech that brought lumps to the throats of many of his listeners. "If I have been true to some of the great causes that I have sought to remain true to, it's been the example of that little fellow that has helped in many ways." He described Pat's fidelity and his uncanny instinct for politics. "He always knew when there had been a fight on. I could tell whether everything had gone well or badly by the rapid movement of his tail and the extent to which he jumped up and down on those occasions."

It was an unusual speech in many ways. King was arguably the most influential Canadian politician of the first half of the 20th century. He had been leader of the Liberal party since 1919 and at the time of the speech was serving his third term as prime minister. He had led Canadians through part of the Great Depression and in 1944 was now leading them through the Second World War. He was respected both at home and abroad, even if his speeches tended to be a little dry and colourless.

This particular speech was in many ways one of his best, showing a warmer, more emotional side of the bachelor prime minister than most people ever encountered. But to those who knew him well, it was no huge surprise. William Lyon Mackenzie King had been unusually devoted to his dog.

Willie, as he was known as a boy and young man, had enjoyed a happy childhood. He was athletic, popular with his schoolmates and a good student. As an adult, he became an adept politician, known especially for his ability as a conciliator. Although he was attracted to women, he never married. He was, however, very close to his parents, especially his mother, Isabel, and to his siblings. Unfortunately, his parents, brother and one sister all died between 1915 and 1922. As prime minister, King might have been the most powerful man in the country, but there was a huge emptiness in his personal life.

That emptiness was partly filled by his friendship with Joan Patteson and her husband, Godfroy. Joan, who was King's confidante and sometimes his hostess at social events, gave King a six-month-old Irish terrier pup in 1924. Typically, Irish terriers are curious, adventurous, affectionate and sometimes mischievous, although it seems Pat was a bit more timid than his brother, Derry, who was Joan's pet. Joan and King frequently walked Pat and Derry together around Kingsmere, the prime minister's country estate, which was located in Gatineau, Quebec.

Until Pat arrived, King had not displayed much interest in animals. However, this quickly changed. King's biographer, C.P. Stacey, wrote, "Dogs are notoriously flatterers of the human ego, and King had a considerable ego to flatter." Before long, the prime minister had become deeply attached to Pat. They walked together every morning and every evening shared a snack—usually oatmeal cookies and Ovaltine. King, who kept a daily diary, mentioned Pat and his brother frequently. On September 19, 1924, he described how much he had enjoyed the company of the "dear little chaps" over the summer. They were:

so knowing & affectionate, Derry full of charm & adventure, Pat very timid but very trustworthy & faithful, loving to romp about together by day—leaping over the fields, chasing each other, biting in a playful way each other's neck & hind leg, loving to jump up & be petted, enjoying sleep above all else, just too sleepy for words at night & early morning, loving to stretch—dear little lads, joyous companions.

King's delight in young Pat continued when he moved back to Laurier House in Ottawa on September 28. That first night in the house, Pat slept beside King's bed. "He was sensitive & timid as could be," wrote King, "but I comforted him, and he kept at my side while at breakfast, while writing, and during lunch."

Disaster struck on the afternoon of September 29. While King was out on government business, a member of his staff took Pat for a walk. Somehow, the pup managed to get his head out of his collar and he ran off. "It was a wet dreary day, the worst we have had," King later wrote. "My heart aches for the little lad, poor little thing, so timid & alone. It has saddened me beyond words."

Despite his worries, King obviously could not ignore his political responsibilities. The next day, he headed off to Port Arthur and Fort William (now Thunder Bay). Although he slept reasonably well, his thoughts kept returning to the nine-month-old pup. "I see his little shrinking form . . . so timid with strangers, so full of confidence when beside me.

If it were a little child that was lost I could hardly feel worse. The grief I feel for little Pat is only equaled by the indignation I felt at Dewett's stupidity & disobedience of orders."

He prayed for Pat's return, and the next day his prayers were answered. A telegram arrived announcing that Pat had been found. Although he was "delighted" with the news, the prime minister had difficulty shaking off the sadness he had felt at Pat's disappearance.

His bond with Pat was strong, and King frequently wrote about their relationship: the joy of coming home to an exuberant greeting from Pat; or the dog's habit of sleeping in the prime minister's bed. There were occasional problems, as with any pup, and once or twice King banished Pat from the house, sending him away for further training.

One of these incidents occurred in February 1925. Whatever the problem was, it could not have been serious, for on February 17 King received word that Pat had won first prize in the novice class at an Ottawa dog show. The win made the newspapers and delighted King, who wrote, "It is amusing he was 'banished' as a punishment & exhibited without [my] knowledge, carrying off first prize." The prime minister also noted wryly that a wolfhound named Mackenzie King had won first prize in another class.

Like many who grew up in the Victorian age, King was a man of faith whose religion affected many aspects of his daily life, including his relationship with his pet. Although he was brought up as a Presbyterian, King's spiritual beliefs had become rather unconventional by the time he was in his 30s. He saw signs and omens everywhere, particularly in certain numbers or the placement of hands on the clock. He also believed he was guided by the spirits of the dead, including not only his mother but also Sir Wilfrid Laurier, whom he had succeeded as Liberal leader. He was certain that those who had gone beyond took an active interest in his daily activities and reached out to him in various ways. King was convinced that it was their influence that had brought Pat into his life.

The prime minister also thought that his mother could provide comfort from beyond the grave. After Pat's sudden disappearance in 1924, King found solace in a dream in which he had seen and kissed his mother. And, as usual, King believed she had interceded with God on his behalf. Once, when he was kneeling in prayer before his mother's portrait, Pat licked his feet. King commented on this in his diary, adding, "I sometimes think he is a comforter dear mother has sent to me, he is filled with her spirit of patience and tenderness & love."

Sometimes King described the dog as "almost human," but more often he referred to Pat as an angel. One typical entry from July 7, 1939, described Pat as "a god-sent little angel in the guise of a dog . . . asking only to be near one and to share the companionship of perfect trust." King was so convinced of the dog's angelic nature that he often kept him near when he prayed. Not only did the prime minister pray for guidance in his professional and personal life, he also asked for favours. When Derry, Pat's brother, was seriously ill in 1934, King knelt with Pat beside him, near the armchair in which his mother once sat, and asked God to send the spirit of Dr. Louis Pasteur to assist the veterinarian who was treating Derry.

Derry's death on August 23, 1940, not only saddened King, but made him realize that Pat was slowing down and aging. The dog was buried at Kingsmere, and the prime minister and Joan Patteson agreed that Pat would eventually be buried alongside him. Pat survived for nearly another year, although he was deaf, barely able to see and very sick. When King returned from a trip to British Columbia, he realized how ill the dog was. Immediately, he was reminded of another sad homecoming, this one in December 1917, after a general election had taken him away from his terminally ill mother. Isabel King had insisted that her son put his political career first and he had complied. But she died before he returned home, and for the rest of his life King felt guilty about having been absent during her final moments. The knowledge that Pat was close to death brought the memories flooding back. "I cried very hard as I realized it could not be long before his little spirit, his brave, noble spirit would have taken its flight, but my tears were mostly of gratitude for God's mercy in so guiding my steps as to bring me home in time."

King described his pet's final days in his 1944 anniversary

King named all of his dogs "Pat." The first Pat was a gift from the Pattesons in 1924. He lived for 17 years. The second Pat was acquired in 1941, but died only six years later. The third Pat was acquired in the mid-1940s; he survived King and was given to family members after King's death.

speech, heralding Pat's intrepid nature. "What impressed me so much was that as he aged, little by little, no longer able to come downstairs, he would be waiting at the top of the stairs, and then after, when he was not able to come to the top of the stairs, I would find him in his little basket wide awake but waiting just to have a word of good-night."

During the summer of 1941, King told his audience, he prepared to leave Ottawa for several weeks in the Canadian west. Just before his departure, he had a heart-to-heart talk with Pat. "I made him promise that no matter how hard the struggle might be, he would stick it out until I got back. I got back one morning, and it was afternoon when I saw him and as I came near the little chap raised up on his feet, wagged his tail, and he finally collapsed. I took him in my arms and he went to sleep." What King did not tell his audience in his 1944 speech, but recorded in his diary, was that he sang hymns and prayed as he held the dog. It was July 15, 1941.

Stories about Pat's passing appeared in several newspapers. Writing in the *Victoria Times*, Bruce Hutchison said, "He was a more familiar figure in Ottawa than many politicians and, I fancy, knew a great deal more . . . Laurier House will be a lonely, gloomy place without him." Other writers described how often King and Pat had been photographed together and how the dog usually accompanied the prime minister when he voted at civic, provincial and Dominion elections. "Pat was one of the best known members of the prime minister's household," wrote H.R. Armstrong in the *Toronto Star*, "and a favorite with neighbors and children."

Just as King and Joan had planned, Pat was laid to rest beside his brother at Kingsmere. On December 31, as he reviewed the previous year, King confided to his diary:

> The event that touched me most deeply of all was perhaps the death of little Pat. Our years together, and particularly our months in the early spring and summer, have been a true spiritual pilgrimage. That little dog has taught me how to live, and also how to look forward, without concern, to the arms that will be around me when I, too, pass away. We shall all be together in the Beyond. Of that I am perfectly sure.

If King needed further convincing, it came through séances. For years he had been visiting mediums who claimed to put him in touch with the spirits of the dead. Some time after Pat's death, King and Joan Patteson attended a séance. The medium informed the prime minister, "Your sister is here, and she has a beautiful dog with her. The dog doesn't seem to have been very long over there." At another séance, King received messages from both his parents, who told him that Pat was happy to be back with Derry and the two brothers were busy hunting rabbits and squirrels. Joan Patteson, who apparently was not as serious about the séances as the prime minister, commented, "I hope there are no cats in heaven—it would be hell if it were."

Meanwhile, Joan helped ease King's loss with another dog. She had actually acquired another Irish terrier after Derry's death. Whether she intended to keep the dog for herself or give him to King is not clear, but after Pat died, the three-year-old became a regular visitor in the prime minister's household and was named Pat II. By September, King was commenting that Pat II seemed to miss him when he was away. By October, the dog was staying permanently with him.

King became quite fond of "the other Pat," whom he also called "The Little Saint." On Christmas Eve 1944, just before going to bed, he talked to Pat II as the dog sat in his basket. "We spoke together of the Christ-child and the animals in the crib," he wrote in his diary. The Second World War was still going on, and if anyone had read King's diary at the time, they might have wondered about the prime minister's sanity.

The war ended in 1945, but King's private notes continued to reflect his unusual attitude toward his dogs. In 1947, when King George VI proposed awarding the prime minister the Order of Merit, Mackenzie King must have realized that it was a high honour: only 24 people belonged to the Order at any one time, and no Canadian had ever been admitted. King hesitated, partly because he was not a great believer in titles, and partly because he thought Pat II, who had recently died of cancer, deserved the medal more than he did. "And then came the thought of the other little Pat," wrote King, "who also merited more than I do, and the loyalty of his nature, fidelity and all that counts for most." Eventually, King decided to accept the medal and said nothing about the dogs.

One more dog came into King's life. Pat III was a gift from King's secretary, J.E. Handy. King was pleased, but never became quite as attached to this dog. His own health was deteriorating. On July 22, 1950, William Lyon Mackenzie King, possibly the most eccentric prime minister Canada has ever produced, died. His body was laid to rest at Toronto's Mount Pleasant Cemetery, but if his prayers were answered, his soul went to join his family and his "little angel dogs."

8

Military Mascots

WHEN THE CALGARY HIGHLANDERS WERE sent to England during the Second World War, they brought a little surprise with them. Heather, an Aberdeen terrier, had been raised in Winnipeg by Pipe Sergeant Neil Sutherland and was presented to the pipe band as their mascot. Defying military regulations, members of the pipe band hid the little dog in the bass drum in order to smuggle her into the country.

The word "mascot" did not enter the English language until the late 1880s. Derived from a Provençal word meaning "witch," and popularized by an 1880 comic opera called *La Mascotte*, the word "mascot" became synonymous with a lucky charm or talisman.

Yet mascots have existed in some form for thousands

of years, perhaps since people first walked the earth. Tribal cultures often included totems—animal guardians to whom people turned for guidance and from whom they frequently claimed descent. Often, people hoped to acquire their totem's chief characteristics, such as strength or bravery. In time, entire nations adopted totems or mascots, such as the Canadian beaver or the eagle of ancient Rome and the United States of America.

Like national symbols, military mascots take on a special meaning, helping to foster unity within a regiment or a ship's crew. For soldiers or sailors on active service, mascots also carry a reminder of home. Animals can frequently provide a welcome diversion from danger or boredom, especially if they are young or playful.

Mascots may also serve a practical role, such as controlling rats and mice on board a ship. Harry B. Barrett, who served on HMCS *Assiniboine* during the Second World War, recalled the ship's mascot, Able-Bodied Sea Cat, in his memoirs. When the *Assiniboine* visited Ireland, A.B. Sea Cat became pregnant. As her delivery date neared, she started looking for a suitable place to give birth. Every time a locker opened, she peered in with interest.

One night, as Harry came off watch, he found his locker open. When he took a closer look, he saw that A.B. Sea Cat had given birth to five kittens, all of them cleaned up and sleeping on his best bell-bottomed trousers. What really surprised him was that just off to one side of the kittens was "a neat row of five straight tiny tails, the blood scarcely dry."

Sometime in early life, A.B. Sea Cat had lost her tail. No one was quite sure how, but she apparently regarded tails as completely abnormal, and when her kittens arrived with strange little appendages on their back ends, she bit each one off. That story probably delighted the *Assiniboine*'s crew for years afterward.

Mascots could also be morale builders. In 1949, the British ship *Amethyst* was held captive by Communist rebels on China's Yangtze River. Several of the men were wounded, as was Simon, the ship's cat. In spite of his injuries, Simon continued with his duties, killing a rat a day. Not only did this bolster the men's spirits, it also helped maintain their precious supplies of food until the siege ended more than three months later.

While most mascots were chosen deliberately, in some instances animals become mascots by chance. In September 1944, the 8th Princess Louise Hussars were on the front lines near Coriano, Italy. The countryside was devastated as Allied and German forces fought for two weeks. Civilians fled for whatever safety they could find, abandoning their farm animals in the process.

As the fighting continued, dead and dying animals became a common sight. On the night of September 15, a group of mechanics and fitters were working on a disabled tank when they heard a scream. Not quite sure whether it was animal or human, they investigated. A young foal, no more than three or four months old, was standing near the body of her mother. The mare had been dead for some time, but the bay filly had worn a path around her mother, unwilling to leave her main source of food and comfort. Already half-starved, she had cried out in pain and terror when wounded in the stomach and legs.

The soldiers brought the little horse to the medic on duty. Although the wounds were not serious, the heat and ever-present flies threatened to cause serious infection, so the foal was treated with antiseptic powder and bandaged up.

Most of the Hussars were too involved in the battle to give much thought to the young horse. But the mechanics and fitters, who were responsible for keeping vehicles and tanks in good repair, had a little more time on their hands. They took on the job of caring for the foal, whom they named Princess Louise, after the daughter of Queen Victoria who had become the regiment's patron in 1882.

The 8th Hussars were once a cavalry unit, with roots stretching back to the time of the American Revolution. In addition, many of the men came from rural New Brunswick. It was natural, therefore, that they should take an interest in the young horse, an interest that was supported by some of the commanding officers. She became a great favourite of the regiment that had once been known as the "Iron Horse."

Every time the regiment moved, they hid Princess Louise.

When the Hussars were ordered to Marseilles, France, a three-ton truck was fitted with a hidden stall, and Princess Louise accompanied the regiment. She travelled with the men through France into Belgium and the Netherlands, until the end of the war.

Then serious problems arose. There were not enough ships to carry troops to Canada, and Princess Louise had to be left behind when the Hussars returned home. After the men reached New Brunswick in January 1946, they did their best to make speedy arrangements for the horse's journey to Canada.

It took a few weeks, but in March she sailed from the Netherlands to New York City, where one of the Hussars, Trooper E.A. Jackson, met her. Together they boarded a train for Saint John, New Brunswick.

Princess Louise was welcomed as warmly as any returning soldier. A huge crowd turned out to see her parade down the street, accompanied by a brass band. She was presented with several service medals, including the 1939–1945 Star, the Italy Star, the France and Germany Star, the Canadian Volunteer Service Medal and, in recognition of the injuries she had received in Italy, three wound stripes. Since she was technically still an Italian citizen, Princess Louise was also given her naturalization papers. The celebration continued in Hampton, where she was made a free woman of the village, a historic right that entitled her "to roam at will over hill and vale and partake of that which she pleaseth." In addition, Princess Louise was made a member of the local branch of the Royal Canadian Legion.

As regimental mascot, Princess Louise participated in many ceremonies and parades and was introduced to dozens of dignitaries. She eventually produced three offspring, including Princess Louise II. In 1973, at the age of 29, she died and was buried near the Hampton cenotaph.

Another regiment with a connection to Princess Louise had an even more unusual pet. In 1945, the Argyll and Sutherland Highlanders of Canada (Princess Louise) were stationed in Germany. Members of the Hamilton, Ontario, regiment included two cooks: Corporal Joe Riley and Private Bill Stewart. At a farmhouse in the countryside they found two young goslings and made pets of them.

The birds accompanied the regiment everywhere, and the soldiers fed them scraps from the kitchen. After one was accidentally killed by a truck, the Argylls took special care of the survivor. He was named Private Tucker and was given a regimental number and an identity disc, which he wore around his neck. Legend has it that since he had a regimental number, Private Tucker was also being paid and spent his earnings buying drinks for his soldier friends.

Private Tucker went to the Netherlands with the regiment, which was later posted to Berlin as part of the postwar army of occupation. The men realized that Tucker could not accompany them, but they also knew that if he was left behind he would probably be turned into someone's dinner.

Wanting to save him from that fate, they arranged to have him killed as gently as possible and his body stuffed. Once the taxidermist had done his job, Private Tucker was to be returned to the regiment.

But the Argyll and Sutherland Highlanders moved to Germany before their mascot was delivered. Private Tucker's whereabouts remained a mystery for three years. Then in April 1948, a parcel arrived at the Hamilton home of John Farmer, a former Argylls major who had never encountered Tucker. He had been wounded and evacuated before the bird joined the regiment.

It did not take long for other members of the regiment to fill in the major. At first, Farmer kept Tucker beside his mantelpiece. Years later, his wife, Roma, told *Hamilton Spectator* reporter Paul Wilson, "Our cat Duppie loved to poke him on the head. It made him sway. He was very lifelike."

Private Tucker stayed with the Farmers until 1955, when John was transferred to Galt. Feeling that the bird belonged with the regiment, the Farmers turned him over to the Argylls. A glass display case was constructed, and Private Tucker was installed in the Sergeants' Mess at the Hamilton Armoury. Today, he is part of the Argylls' regimental museum, although he has now been promoted to honorary sergeant.

Mascots frequently serve ceremonial purposes, and this is certainly the case with two goats, David and Batisse. David the Goat—or, more correctly, David IX—is the mascot of the Fort Henry Guards in Kingston. The fort, now a national historic site, was home to the 23rd Regiment of Foot (Royal Welch Fusiliers) in 1842 and 1843. That regiment had a goat named Bill, and to recreate the historic period, the modern fort also has a goat—David.

The original David was a white Saanen goat donated to Fort Henry in 1953 by the Saint David Society of Toronto. Named in honour of the patron saint of Wales, the homeland of the Royal Welch Fusiliers, the society has donated all nine goats to Fort Henry over the past half century. David IX walks around the fort daily, much to the delight of visitors. He also participates in parades and other events, and every day at 3 p.m. he is inspected by the officer of the day.

The Fort Henry Guard is not the only regiment boasting a goat as a mascot. Batisse is the mascot of the Royal 22nd—a French-Canadian regiment formed during the First World War. Still active, the 22nd (or Van Doos) is stationed at the Quebec Citadel, a noted historic site and tourist attraction. The original Batisse was given to the regiment by Queen Elizabeth II in 1955, but his ancestry can be traced back to a Tibetan goat presented to Queen Victoria by the Shah of Persia (Iran) in 1844. All eight of the 22nd regiment's mascots can be traced to that exotic animal. Although 1994 budget cuts temporarily threatened the career of Batisse VII, today his successor is still participating in various regimental parades and functions. In addition, inspired by Batisse, the Quebec Citadelles hockey team has adopted a billy goat as its mascot.

One mascot that has earned a special place in history is Gander. During the Second World War, Gander was an important air base in Newfoundland used by British, Canadian and US air forces, as well as by the Canadian military.

The Haydens, one of the families who lived at the base, owned a large Newfoundland dog named Pal. Like most of his breed, Pal was friendly and playful, but he was also a bit of a discipline problem. He repeatedly got into trouble for confusing pilots as they came in for a landing. Many of them thought he was a bear. And one day, while playing with some children, he accidentally scratched a girl's face.

Even though Pal was popular with local kids who loved having him pull them along on sleds, the Haydens were worried that he might do some serious damage. As a result, he was offered to the Royal Rifles of Canada, who were stationed on the base. Renamed Gander, the dog soon became the regimental mascot.

But in 1941, the Royal Rifles got word that they were shipping out to Hong Kong. The war in the Pacific was not going well. Japan had invaded China, and Britain was concerned that the colony of Hong Kong would fall into enemy hands. Along with the Winnipeg Grenadiers, the Royal Rifles were sent to defend the colony. As soon as the regiment found out they were heading overseas, they promoted Gander to the rank of sergeant and took him along. It was a fateful decision.

The regiments arrived three weeks before the Japanese attacked Hong Kong on December 8. The battle continued for 17 days before the colony fell on Christmas Day. During the brutal fighting, some 290 men died. But the numbers would most certainly have been higher had it not been for Gander's presence.

One day, when Japanese troops landed near a section of the beach defended by the Royal Rifles, Gander raced out, barking and trying to bite the invaders' legs. On another occasion, invading troops were approaching a spot where there were a number of wounded soldiers. Gander again charged the enemy. Although they could have shot the big dog, the Japanese changed their route, and the wounded soldiers were safe for a time.

Later in the battle, Gander was again with a group of wounded soldiers when a grenade was tossed into their vicinity. Before any of the men could react, Gander grabbed the grenade and charged toward the enemy. He was killed in the explosion, but the men were saved.

For more than 50 years, Gander's bravery was known only to a handful of people. Then Eileen Elms, the sister of the girl whom Gander had scratched, talked about him to local historian Frank Tibbo. The dog's story was widely publicized, and in 2000, when the Hong Kong Veterans of Canada held a reunion in Fredericton, New Brunswick, Gander was posthumously awarded the Dickin Medal.

Established during the Second World War by British animal lover and founder of the People's Dispensary for Sick Animals (PDSA), Maria Dickin, the medal has been called the Victoria Cross for animals. Its purpose was to recognize animals who had displayed "conspicuous gallantry and devotion to duty" while attached to military or civil defence units. Between 1943 and 1949, 54 animals received the medal, including Simon, the ship's cat aboard HMS *Amethyst*. After 1949, no medals were awarded until Gander's story came to light.

The Dickin medal is a large bronze medallion hanging from a striped ribbon. On it is inscribed the phrase, "We also serve," a reminder that humans are not the only creatures who sacrifice themselves in armed conflicts.

9

Valiant but Voiceless

FOR CENTURIES, DOGS AND HORSES have worked along-side humans, carrying their burdens, offering mute acts of heroism and sometimes unwittingly sacrificing their lives for their owners. As hunters, herders and guardians, dogs continue to fill the roles that have traditionally made them indispensable. Horses, too, have been integral to North America's history, undertaking essential tasks from plowing to policing.

On February 24, 2006, after Toronto police constable Kevin Bradfield gave him a warning, an angry driver deliberately drove into Bradfield's horse, Brigadier. Like many mounted officers, Bradfield had bonded closely with Brigadier, whom many called the "Gentle Giant." Bradfield later recalled that whenever he visited the horse barn, Brigadier watched every move he made.

When the vehicle slammed into him, it broke two of Brigadier's legs. Although Bradfield was thrown into the street, breaking his ribs and suffering neck and leg injuries, the Belgian-cross had saved his rider's life by taking most of the vehicle's impact. Brigadier, however, was in such pain that he had to be shot at the scene.

Brigadier's death resulted in an outpouring of grief all over North America, especially among police officers. Some 800 people turned out for the horse's memorial service in March, including mounted police officers from across Canada and the United States. Still recuperating, Constable Bradfield attended the poignant ceremony. "Today I'm grateful to be able to say goodbye to my partner, and tell him that being in a saddle will never be the same."

In memory of Brigadier, the Toronto Police Service and the Ontario Veterinary College created a special memorial fund. There were some who wondered whether the fuss was necessary, but there was no doubt in the minds of mounted police officers. As Staff Inspector Bill Wardle told a reporter, "We do consider our mounts family and we mourn their loss appropriately."

A similar outpouring of grief occurred in 1998 when an Edmonton police dog was killed on duty. Caesar was a Rottweiler, a five-year-old police service dog. Tom Braid, a photographer with the *Edmonton Sun*, knew Caesar well.

Although he was not intimidated by guns, Caesar had a fear of heights. In fact, he was so terrified by high places that he shook like a leaf when Braid tried to photograph him on an overpass. But he still carried out his duties with enthusiasm, and when Caesar wasn't working, Braid recalled that the dog was "a docile friendly family pet that would lick you silly if you let him." His gentleness made him perfect for visits to area schools, where he and his handler, Constable Randy Goss, were always warmly welcomed.

On June 23, 1998, an armed man was seen in an athletic field bordering Bishop Saveryn Catholic Elementary School and two other schools. The 20-year-old man, who was firing into the air when the police arrived, ignored repeated orders to put down his weapons. Constable Goss released Caesar, who charged at the man's back, ready to take him down. Seconds before the dog reached him, the man turned and fired point blank into Caesar's head, before aiming his gun at the police. The man was then shot by officers, handcuffed and taken to hospital.

Meanwhile, Constable Goss knelt down beside the dying dog, weeping and pressing his face into Caesar's side as he died. It was a devastating blow for the young officer, who had been caring for Caesar since he was 10 weeks old. The loss was also felt throughout the community, especially among the schoolchildren who had met and admired Caesar. Soon after the news was announced, officers at the police kennels received hundreds of calls, messages of condolence, visits, cards and flowers. Police spokesman Kelly Gordon summed up the community's reaction with a few well-chosen words: "This may be just a dog to some people, but as a member of the police service it's essentially a police officer, a trained police officer, and one of our own has been killed in the line of duty." Caesar was subsequently named Ralston Purina Service Dog of the Year.

Over the years, there have also been many animals that needed no training at all to behave heroically. Among them was Samantha, known as Sam, a German shepherd who belonged to Brian Holmes and Michelle Pilon of Penetanguishene, Ontario. On a bitter day in February 1993, Sam, who enjoyed the cold, was outside doing her rounds. When Michelle looked out to check on her, she saw Sam at the end of the drive, accompanied by a small child. The little boy's arms were tightly wound around the dog's neck and Sam was moving slowly so the child could keep up with her. As Michelle approached, Samantha turned to lick the boy's face.

There were no houses nearby, and the child was not dressed properly for the cold. He had put a light jacket over his pajamas and had taken his toy car out for a spin. Whether Samantha found him or he approached her after realizing he was lost is anybody's guess. But Sam's friendliness got the child to safety in the nick of time. He was already suffering from the early stages of hypothermia.

Meanwhile, the boy's frantic father was searching for his son. His wife had just given birth to a new baby, and the man had fallen asleep from exhaustion. While his father slept, three-year-old Donald decided to visit the hospital. He had been outside for at least 90 minutes in freezing temperatures when Samantha found him. As a result of her role in the boy's rescue, Samantha was named Ontario SPCA Hero of the Year a few months later. Whether Samantha was motivated by maternal instinct, or just a sense that something was not right, her actions made a vital difference in one family's life.

In June 2004, the actions of three other dogs prevented a bloody massacre that might have devastated several families. It was June 23, and James Paul Stanson had driven from New Brunswick to Toronto. He was depressed, suffering from heart trouble and unemployed. A quiet loner, he had brought his dog with him and later checked the dog into a kennel in Newmarket.

But Stanson was also carrying a deadly cargo in his car, including rifles equipped with telescopes, a 9-mm semi-automatic handgun, nearly 6,300 rounds of ammunition, a machete and several knives. He reached the Beaches area in the city's east end and was thinking about shooting people at random. This way, he knew he would be sent to prison for life.

Stanson was about to get his guns ready when Elvis, a local border collie, ran up to him with a Frisbee in his mouth, begging to play. Even though the man was a stranger, Elvis was insistent, and Stanson, a dog lover, tugged at the Frisbee. Elvis tugged back, then wandered off. Temporarily diverted from his plans, Stanson roamed the neighbourhood a bit. Kristina Kyser was out walking with her new baby and her dog, Dante. The four-year-old husky–Australian shepherd cross spotted a large man in a windbreaker and ran up to greet him. Stanson patted Dante and then continued on his way. As he walked through the neighbourhood, Stanson encountered Cisco, an Australian shepherd, whom he also patted.

A short time later, Stanson drove his car to a grocery store and turned himself in to the first police officer he encountered. Later, another officer, Toronto Police detective Nick Ashley, told reporters, "It's scary how close it could have been. He happens to be a pet lover, and decided that since there was such a nice dog in the area, that people were too nice and he wasn't going to carry out his plan."

It took a while to sort out just which dog Stanson was talking about. Gradually, residents of the Beaches pieced it together, and a few months later the Humane Society of Canada recognized all three dogs with a presentation of the Animal Heroes Award. In summing up the reason for the presentation, Humane Society director Michael O'Sullivan said, "There is no doubt in my mind at all, that the overall atmosphere of friendly dogs and people in the Beaches helped save the day."

Almost a century earlier, another group of dogs had saved the life of one very special man. English medical missionary

Wilfred Grenfell joined the Royal National Mission to Deep Sea Fishermen in 1888 and came to Newfoundland, where many of the outports were accessible only by boat in the warmer months or by dogsled in the winter. Grenfell established nursing stations, an orphanage and a hospital. By 1908, his hospital in St. Anthony's was well known.

On Easter Sunday of that year, Grenfell was called to treat a seriously ill patient who lived about 100 kilometres south of St. Anthony's. The young man had recently undergone surgery. Complications developed and infection had set in. Realizing there was no time to lose, Grenfell packed surgical instruments, drugs and other supplies. Being familiar with April weather in Newfoundland, he knew he would probably get wet somewhere along the way and added extra clothing, including oilskins and outer garments. He took a rifle, compass and axe in case of emergency, loaded up a dog sled and set out along the frozen coast.

Grenfell was very proud of the team, admiring their strength, their wisdom and their beauty. He described them as:

> Brin, the cleverest leader on the coast; Doc, a large, gentle beast, the backbone of the team for power; Spy, a wiry, powerful, black and white dog; Moody, a lop-eared black-and-tan . . . a plodder that never looked behind him; Watch, the youngster of the team, long-legged and speedy, with great liquid eyes and a Gordon-setter coat; Sue, a large, dark

Eskimo, the image of a great black wolf, with her sharp-pointed and perpendicular ears; Jerry . . . so affectionate that her overtures of joy had often sent me sprawling on my back; Jack, a jet-black, gentle-natured dog . . . that always ran next the sledge, and never looked back but everlastingly pulled straight ahead, running always with his nose to the ground.

He set out with the two messengers who had summoned him to his ailing patient, but their dogs were tired from the journey to St. Anthony's. So, in a very short time, Grenfell and his team were some distance ahead.

The first day passed without incident. Grenfell and the others made over 30 kilometres by nightfall and stayed in a village. The following morning, the weather changed. A northeasterly wind brought in fog and rain, creating treacherous travelling conditions.

This time, Grenfell sent the other two men ahead with their team, agreeing to meet them in a log cabin in the woods. By the time he started out to join them, it was raining. The first leg of his journey took him along the coast, where the ice was already beginning to crack and pile up. Searching for the quickest and safest path, Grenfell headed for an island about 5 kilometres offshore, which at that time of year was connected to land by an ice bridge. From there, he headed for a rocky point about 6.5 kilometres away. Before setting out, he scanned the horizon, checking the ice. It seemed rough but solid, and, eager to complete his journey as quickly as possible, he decided to risk the route.

At first everything went well. Then, when Grenfell was about a half kilometre from landfall, the wind changed, switching around to the west. Grenfell realized that the consistency of the ice beneath him had changed, too. The ice was breaking up into pans or slabs, none larger than three metres square, and the wind was driving it toward the open sea. Moments later, his dogsled was sinking into the icy water.

As the komatik with all his supplies went down, Grenfell grabbed his knife. Flashing through his mind was the memory of another fisherman who had drowned a few months earlier after becoming tangled in the traces of his dogsled. Grenfell quickly cut the lines but held onto the trace attached to Brin, the lead dog.

The ice was like molasses, too thick to swim through, too thin to stand upon. When Brin clambered onto a solid piece of ice, Grenfell sensed there was hope for survival. Still holding onto the dog's line, he began to pull himself slowly toward the ice pan. Suddenly Brin shook free of his harness and the line went slack. Grenfell managed to catch the trace of another dog who was close to the ice pan, and, after struggling for several minutes, he was able to climb up beside Brin. Then, one by one, he hauled the other dogs out of the icy water.

They were no longer in immediate danger of drowning, but Grenfell and his dogs were stranded on a tiny ice pan, soaking wet. Over the next few hours, he removed the traces from his dogs, retied them in a long line, and persuaded the animals to move toward a larger piece of ice. But they were still too far out to make it to the safety of shore.

Grenfell thought he was too far from the shoreline to be seen by anyone. Even if by some miracle he was spotted, it would be almost impossible for a boat to reach him through the shifting ice. With little hope of immediate rescue, and faced with the very real danger of freezing to death over-night, Grenfell formed a desperate plan. He decided to kill three of his dogs.

> Unwinding the sealskin traces from my waist, round which I had wound them to keep the dogs from eating them, I made a slip-knot, passed it over the first dog's head, tied it round my foot close to his neck, threw him on his back and stabbed him in the heart. Poor beast! I loved him like a friend—a beautiful dog—but we could not all hope to live. In fact, I had no hope any of us would, at that time, but it seemed better to die fighting.

Moody, Watch and Spy were sacrificed. Grenfell spent the night cuddled into Doc, the largest of the dogs, with the skins of the three dead dogs wrapped around him like blankets.

Grenfell survived the night. The next day, the pan be-gan to drift toward land. Grenfell lashed together the frozen legs of the dead dogs, attached his shirt to them, and waved this makeshift flag in the direction of land. In his weakened state, he found it so heavy that he had to rest frequently. Every time he did, Doc walked up to him, licked his face and then walked to the edge of the ice pan and back to him, "as if to say, 'Why don't you come along?'"

As the hours passed, Grenfell decided he would have to kill another dog. He had not eaten since the previous morning, and while he was not prepared to devour his dogs, he had heard of people surviving similar ordeals by drinking animal blood. But he was no longer sure he had the strength to try. As it turned out, he did not have to resort to this drastic measure. Someone had spotted Grenfell and his dogs, and in the face of considerable danger, a group of fishermen rowed out to rescue them.

Grenfell recounted his adventure in a small book, *Adrift on an Ice-Pan*, concluding:

> Jack lies curled up by my feet while I write this short account. Brin is once again leading and lording it over his fellows. Doc and the other survivors are not forgotten, now that we have again returned to the less romantic episodes of a mission hospital life. There stands in our hallway a bronze tablet to the memory of three noble dogs, Moody, Watch and Spy, whose lives were given for mine on the ice. In my home in England my brother has placed a duplicate tablet and has added these words, "Not one

of them is forgotten before your Father which is in heaven." And this I must fully believe to be true.

The sacrifice made by Moody, Watch and Spy was unintentional, like that of police animals killed in action. In doing what they were trained to do, these dogs and horses found themselves in circumstances that ended their lives, often without understanding the dangers they faced. And yet there is something tremendously touching about animals whose devotion to their masters and to their duties brings them face to face with injury or death.

Epilogue

PEOPLE'S LOVE AFFAIR WITH ANIMALS transcends space and time. Through the centuries we have shared our lives with dogs, cats, horses and more exotic creatures, including monkeys and elephants. We have been amazed by their playfulness, overwhelmed by their devotion and courage, and awed by an intelligence that is both very different from, and yet as penetrating as our own.

Writing about his beaver kittens, Grey Owl compared them to little people from another planet whose language we have yet to learn. Anyone who has spent time in the company of animals, observing them closely, knows the same can be said of many creatures. We are all caught in the same web of creation. And because we are interconnected in so many ways, pets, as much as people, are a precious part of our heritage.

Select Bibliography

Quoted material in this book comes from numerous sources, both historical and more current. The author gratefully acknowledges the following primary sources:

Campbell, Patrick. *Travels in the Interior Inhabited Parts of North America in the Years 1791 and 1792*. Toronto: Champlain Society, 1937.

Carr, Emily. *The Complete Writings of Emily Carr*. Vancouver: Douglas & McIntyre; Seattle: University of Washington Press, 1997.

Grenfell, Wilfred Thomason. *Adrift on An Ice-Pan*. Toronto: Copp Clark; Houghton Mifflin, 1909.

Grey Owl. *Pilgrims of the Wild*. London, Ontario: Gatefold Books, 1980.

Jolly, W.P. *Jumbo*. London: Constable, 1976.

King, W.L.M. *The Mackenzie King diaries, 1893–1931: the complete manuscript entries with accompanying typewritten transcription and other original typewritten journals*. Toronto: University of Toronto Press, ca. 1973.

Marchand, Leslie. A. *Byron: A Biography*. New York: Alfred A. Knopf, 1957.

Shushkewic, Val. *The Real Winnie: A One-of-a-Kind Bear*. Toronto: Natural Heritage/Natural History, 2003.

Index

Index

Acknowledgements

The author gratefully acknowledges the assistance of Rick Seager, curator at the Argyll and Sutherland Highlanders of Canada (Princess Louise's) museum in Hamilton, as well as the following Internet sources: *Dictionary of Canadian Biography* online at www.biographi.ca; Linda Hersey's "A Royal Filly" from *Legion Magazine* online at www.legionmagazine. com/features/memoirspilgrimages/03-09.asp; www.pulse24.com/News/Top_Story/20060306-005/page.asp for quotes about police horse Brigadier; Hendersonville Police Department Home Page at www.hendersonville-pd.org/caesar.html; *The Globe and Mail*, June 28, 2004; and the Humane Society of Canada at www.humanesociety.com. The author wishes to acknowledge the dedication and persistence of editors Jane Chamberlin Grove, Lesley Cameron and Lesley Reynolds.

About the Author

Cheryl MacDonald is a full-time writer and historian who has been writing about Canadian history for more than 30 years. Her historical articles have appeared in *The Beaver*, *Maclean's*, the *Hamilton Spectator* and the *Old Farmer's Almanac*. Cheryl has also written, co-authored or published about 40 books on the history of Ontario and Canada, including the Amazing Stories titles *Niagara Daredevils*, *Great Canadian Love Stories*, *Christmas in Ontario*, *Laura Secord* and *Deadly Women of Ontario*. She lives in rural Nanticoke, Ontario, with a household of pets, including Louie the Labrador; Sophie, a senior Siamese; and the Orangetigger twins, Arnold and Samantha.

More Great Books in the Amazing Stories Series

Inspiring Animal Tales

Heartwarming Stories of
Courage and Devotion

Roxanne Willems Snopek

(ISBN 978-1-894974-77-6)

The touching stories in this collection provide hope to everyone who has
ever wondered if they could overcome a difficult start. The answer is yes,
with a little help from an animal friend, and a good measure of love, trust
and dedication. From National Service Dogs to dogs with disabilities,
from donkeys to parrots, the animals in this book have all brought joy
and hope into people's lives. Their stories are truly inspiring.

Also by Roxanne Willems Snopek:

Wildlife in the Kitchen: And Other Great Animal Tales
(ISBN 978-1-554390-08-3)

Visit www.heritagehouse.ca to see the entire list of books in this series.

More Great Books in the Amazing Stories Series

Rescue Dogs

Crime and Rescue Canines
in the Canadian Rockies

Dale Portman

(ISBN 978-1-894974-78-3)

This collection of crime and rescue stories by a retired park warden and dog trainer highlights the vital role dogs play in saving lives, upholding the law and recovering bodies. Portman describes the escapades of Canadian Rockies park warden Alfie Burstrom and his canine partner, Ginger—the first certified avalanche search team in North America— as well as his own adventures tracking down criminals and missing persons with his German shepherd, Sam. These stories will give you a new appreciation of working dogs.

Also by Dale Portman:

Riding on the Wild Side: Tales of Adventure in the Canadian West
(ISBN 978-1-894974-80-6)

Visit www.heritagehouse.ca to see the entire list of books in this series.